IT'S YOUR
LIFE...

LIVE IT AND LOVE IT

IT'S YOUR
LIFE...

LIVE IT AND LOVE IT

BILL ARMSTRONG
...the Sage of Sedona

Aventine Press

Published by Aventine Press
1023 4th Ave #204
San Diego CA, 92101

ISBN: 1-59330-532-X
Printed in the United States of America

To Mike . . . .

May your Earth Walk be long, happy,
and Prosperous. At each new
Crossroad trust your Intuition !

Expect Miracles !

Best wishes

Bill Armstrong

Table of Contents

When the pen takes over...

Every writer will understand what I mean when I say that there are times when the pen takes over. Often it happens when you are alone with your thoughts. You pick up a pen and words suddenly begin to race across the page. They fairly tumble from the pen onto the paper. When the pen stops writing something special has been created. It is a story, a poem, a song...or just an unusual collection of thoughts. You don't necessarily know where the words came from, or even why they are there, staring back at you from the page.

For me this phenomenon takes place sometimes in the middle of the night. An idea comes to mind that just will not go away. I would much rather sleep, but this persistent and nagging thought will not give me any peace until it is on paper. That is what I am referring to when I speak of stories, or musings that have been given to me. I did not set out to create them, they just appeared out of nowhere. These words would never have made it to the page if the pen had not taken over. And these thoughts--these words--will completely disappear if I do not stop what I am doing and let the pen have its way.

It must be the same for an artist. There must be times when they sit down to work and the brush takes over. Colors leap from the palette and a unique painting becomes an unintended reality. It may not their best work...it may not even be something that will be a big winner in the marketplace, but it will be special and meaningful to someone.

Where does this stuff come from? How do these words and pictures get into the pen or brush in the first place? The only explanation I can offer comes from something Mother Teresa once said. This special lady summed up her work as simply:

"I am but a pencil in the hand of a writing God."

What a powerful thought! But when you think about it, we are all pencils in the hand of our Creator. There are times when each of us has something within us that needs to be expressed. Every one of us has something that must be shared with someone else. It may be a story, a book, a poem, a song...or even a letter that needs to be written for whatever reason. You know what I mean...it is inside of you yearning to be expressed. It needs to be expressed. It must be expressed. For God's sake...let the pen take over.

The Price of Wisdom

A few years ago a traveler journeyed to the top of a mountain in a far off land to meet with a renowned holy man. At the appointed time The Traveler was ushered into a large open area. The Holy Man sat on a pile of thick cushions. He motioned for The Traveler to come forward and sit in front of him. He looked at The Traveler for some time before he spoke in a soft voice. "What is it you seek, my son?" Without hesitation The Traveler replied, "I seek wisdom."

Again he looked at The Traveler in silence for many moments. Then he smiled and said softly, "You have come a great distance and you seek only wisdom?"

"I believe wisdom is a most valuable gift. When one has wisdom he can help many people to find happiness--to find their life's purpose--to live an abundant life."

The Holy Man sat silently for a great while. When he finally spoke his voice was barely audible. "In two days time I am leaving on a long journey. If you wish you may accompany me."

Early on the morning of the second day The Traveler met The Holy Man at the foot of the road leading to the mountaintop. The Traveler had brought enough provisions to last for several weeks and sufficient funds to pay for his lodging. As they began their journey The Traveler realized The Holy Man carried nothing--no food, no coins, no extra clothing. The Traveler assumed at first that The Holy Man might be fasting.

As they walked that day The Holy Man spoke not a word. They traveled in complete silence. At the end of the day The Holy Man left to watch the sunset and to meditate and to pray. The Traveler set about to prepare a portion of his provisions for his evening meal. As he sat down to eat The Holy Man suddenly appeared and sat down in front of The Traveler. He picked up the bowl of food and took a large portion for himself. He laughed and said simply that meditation and prayer gave him a hearty appetite. The Traveler nodded and ate the small portion that remained. Later that evening The Traveler sought lodging at a nearby inn. As he was prepared to retire The Holy Man appeared. Without a word he took the bed, leaving The Traveler to sleep on a small straw mat in the corner of the room.

And so it was each night of the journey. The Traveler prepared the food while The Holy Man left to enjoy a beautiful sunset, to meditate, and to pray. He appeared at mealtime, took the largest portion of the food, and the bed at the inn. Each day of the journey was the same. No conversation...no words of wisdom. The Traveler was left to find some way to stretch his provisions so that they would feed two people, and to find lodging for both of them. The Traveler was never able to enjoy a single sunset. He never had a single moment to meditate or pray. Each day they traveled in complete silence.

When they reached the high country the weather became quite cold. The Traveler noticed The Holy Man had no cloak...The Traveler gave him his. When The Holy Man's sandals broke...The Traveler gave him his. In time The Traveler's provisions were running out, as was his money. But yet each day he managed to scrape together enough to eat and a place to sleep. Throughout the entire journey The Traveler heard not one word of gratitude or appreciation from The Holy Man.

When the journey was at last complete they arrived back at the large open space at the top of the mountain. The Holy Man took his place on the pile of cushions and once there he summoned his students. They quickly arrived and gathered close to him to hear his words. When they were assembled he began to tell them of the journey he had just completed. He spoke at length in glowing terms of the magnificent sunsets he had seen…of the insightful meditations he had experienced…of the great inspirations that he had received while in prayer. The students hung on to his every word. They listened in complete awe as The Holy Man described how his great faith had allowed him to journey with no script nor coin. He was able to travel completely unencumbered with worldly goods and possessions.

They applauded and marveled at his faith. Truly he was a man greatly favored by his God. How else could he have made such a miraculous journey. The Holy Man smiled benevolently and reveled in their adoration.

The Traveler watched them for a time...then he got up and slowly made his way back down the mountain...much wiser than before.

Beggars...or Kings?

One evening when I was standing on a corner waiting for my wife, a beggar approached me. He got my attention immediately. It was an evening in late March. The weather had taken a sudden turn for the worse. The temperature had dropped about thirty degrees in the space of a few hours. Even my topcoat offered scant protection from the wind. And here, standing in front of me was this short, stocky man in a short sleeved tee shirt. At first he spoke so softly I wasn't sure what he said. He asked again, "Sir, can you spare a few bucks? I'm out of work and we need some food."

Without answering I took a few dollars out of my pocket and handed them to him. He thanked me and turned toward the other people who were hurrying home from work. Most brushed past him, but a few paused to give

him some money. After a few minutes he turned
back to me. "Sir, can you spare any more?
I really need some more money." I looked at
him in disbelief; "I just gave you some money!" He looked at me for a moment, "Sorry."
He walked a few yards away and approached
several other people. In a few minutes he
was back. "Sir, please, I really need twenty
bucks to get some food."

I was now getting annoyed. "Buddy, if you
ask me one time I'm going take that money
back!" He looked down at his shabby shoes
and muttered, "Sorry." He turned and hurried
down the street. I saw him several times over
the next few months, but he always seemed to
cross the street or turn down a side street
before he got to me.

About a year or so later, just before we
moved from Pittsburgh, I was heading for a
meeting when he suddenly appeared. As he approached me I impatiently, and I must admit
rudely, prepared to brush him off. "Sorry,
I don't have spare change today." He looked
surprised.

"Oh, no", he said. "You helped me out once
when I really needed help. I just wanted to
tell you that I am working now. I got a good

job. We have a nice little apartment and we are expecting a baby. I just wanted to thank you for your help." He smiled, his countenance seemed somehow softer, more relaxed, happier. He shook my hand and disappeared around the corner. I could only stare after him in stunned disbelief. I admit I felt more than a little ashamed of myself.

Was he a beggar...or a king?

An even stranger situation occurred after we moved to New York. I had an early dentist appointment one morning and I was running late. To make it worse it was raining and there wasn't a taxi in sight. As I raced up the street I heard a voice coming from out of the darkness in front of an abandoned building. "Sir, can you spare some change?"

As I brushed past I grunted, "No, I don't have any change!" For some reason I paused and looked at the man. I froze. It was his eyes. They were bright blue. They were soft, kind...and yet piercing...like no eyes I had ever seen before. They seemed to actually smile at me! I hurried on to my dental appointment. But the entire time I sat in the chair I could not get those eyes out of my mind. I kept thinking about that scripture where The Savior says, "As ye have done to the least of these, my brethren, ye have done it unto me."

I hurried back to that building, but the man was gone. I walked around for several blocks in every direction, but he was not to be found. I never saw him again, but those eyes haunt me. Just as often I remember that scripture and wonder...

Was he a beggar...or a king?

Since that day I have never passed a person asking for help that I haven't made some contribution. And each time I ask myself...

Was he a beggar...or a king?

Should it really matter?

★★★

That I feed the hungry, forgive an insult, and love my enemy—these are great virtues. But what if I should discover that the poorest of the beggars and the most imprudent of offenders are all within me, and that I stand in need of the alms of my own kindness; that I myself am the enemy who must be loved...what then?

C. G. Jung

Table Talk

Scientists have determined that as parents we spend an average of only 14.5 minutes a day talking to our children. But even more distressing is their conclusion that 12.5 minutes of that time is spent pointing out to them what they have done wrong, telling them what they should be doing, and how they should do it. This leaves virtually no time at all for listening--no time for listening while they express what <u>they</u> feel are important issues--no time to listen to their concerns and fears--no time to learn about their problems. When they *are* able to tell us about a problem we tend to give them a stock answer, "Don't hang around with them any more!" "You need to work harder!" "Teachers don't know anything--just go along with them!"

Then when something serious happens we ask aloud, "Where were the parents? How could they let this happen?" Today, with the growth of two income families, a new term has emerged. People now talk about the "quality time" they spend with their children. In what must be considered a very informal survey I asked a number of parents how they defined "quality time". Most could not come up with anything that resembled a well thought out response. Most responded, "Well, its just time I have available to spend with my kids". The definitive word is "available"--it is the time left over after everything else has been taken care of. When asked how often they have real "quality time" with their children, the most common answer was, "Oh, I don't know, at least twice a week."

But the real surprise was their response to the question, "What do you do during your quality time? The two overwhelming responses were, "We go with them to their ball games (dance lessons, gymnastics, etc.), or "We all go to McDonalds!" Shocking isn't it, that parents would actually see having a meal at a fast food restaurant as "quality time"? Several parents said that for their quality time they took their kids with them when they went golfing or bowling. One father said adamantly, "But that is only if he has his homework and his chores done!"   Now I won't dispute that it is possible to spend quality time with a child on a golf course, or at the local bowling alley. But it shouldn't be the only time and place you spend time together.

Millions of parents unselfishly devote time to scouting, coaching Little League, and the like. But in some cases these parents should honestly ask themselves whether this is for the child, or for themselves. Is it an attempt to spend time with your children, or something you personally enjoy doing? And, how much quality time does your child get when your time is split between a dozen or so other children?

No, for your souls to touch you need to spend regular periods of time face-to-face with your children. And you need to learn about what they see as problems and issues. You need to see the world through <u>their</u> eyes.

At a recent workshop I conducted for a group of at-risk teenagers, I noticed one young girl spent the time being "cool". She made few meaningful responses and very little eye contact. She gave the impression she was not the least bit interested in the program. However, about a month later I received an interesting letter from her. She said that

when she got home that day she laid the hand-
outs on the kitchen table. Her father picked
up the material, read it, and asked her about
the program during dinner. The entire family
became so engrossed in their discussion that
they talked for quite some time even after
the table had been cleared. She said this
was the first they had ever discussed anything
of significance at the dinner table. She added that it had become a regular occurrence
and, as a family, they had become closer than
ever before.

That made me think about my own children
and how much I learned about them during the
dinner hour. In today's home environment few
families ever eat dinner together, let alone
around the table.

In many homes the evening meal is eaten
in shifts to accommodate busy schedules, or
television programming. Usually the meal is
consumed in silence around the TV set. As a
result we are missing a great opportunity to
grow as a family unit...to learn to understand one another...to have a time when our
souls can touch!

This brings me to the point of this piece-
-ways to grow the family unit. At least

several times a week make certain the entire family gathers around the dinner table. No TV! No distractions! Just table talk! Talk about any issues of current importance. But let the kids talk. Make sure they take turns, don't let one dominate the discussion. But let them express themselves. When they say something outrageous or something you dispute, don't argue or point out where they are wrong. Instead, in a non-judgmental way, ask them <u>why</u> they feel that way. Their answers will help you understand them better. Are their views well thought out, or are they reflections of what their friends think? Are they deep thinkers, or are their views superficial? Are their views a product of Mr. Rogers...or Jerry Springer?

The information you gather will be extremely helpful as you hone your parenting skills. And incidentally, the ability to listen without being judgmental is a valuable skill at any time, in any place.

The Window

A few years ago I was driving down a dusty road toward an uncertain future, when I came upon an old handmade sign that read:

Ten miles to
THE WINDOW--
See the answer to any problem

A few minutes later I saw another sign:

8 miles to
THE WINDOW--
See the answer to any problem

I was somewhat amused. The sign was crude, almost as if it were made by a child. I could not help but chuckle out loud, "How is it possible that by gazing through a window you could see the answer to any problem?" Surely it was a joke! If only it were that

simple. If only I could resolve my problems,
to know which road to choose, to know for a
certainty that there is some small particle
of happiness and success out there for me--
somewhere.

As if Marsha's sudden request for a divorce
hadn't hit hard enough...then there was the
downsizing at work. What had I done to deserve this? Hadn't I reached a point in life
when things were supposed to be more stable,
to become more settled, dependable? Here I
am, alone, unemployed, driving clear across
the country to take a job with a struggling
young company I know almost nothing about, in
an unfamiliar town, where I don't know a single person. Why? Why am I doing this? What
am I running from? What am I running to?

6 miles to
THE WINDOW--
See the answer to any problem

Did I make the right decision? I'm sure
another job would have turned up. Some companies must be expanding! I've always been
a productive person...well, at least up until the past year or so. And that was only

because of the stress at work...the new own-
ers...the downsizing.   Maybe the cutback
would only be a temporary thing.   Business
will pick up again.   It always has.   They
just over-reacted!   Besides, if they had to
cut somewhere they could have cut some of the
perks the sales people get.   If they had done
their jobs, if *they* had worked harder, there
wouldn't have been any cutbacks.

4 miles to
THE WINDOW--
See the answer to any problem

   What am I running from?   Maybe it was
the unanswered questions on the minds of
all our friends.   "Why <u>did</u> Marsha and I divorce?"   "Whose fault was it?"   "Was there
someone else involved?"   "Was there any hope
of a reconciliation?"   Questions I had no
answers for...what <u>did</u> happen?   Wasn't I at-
tentive enough?   She should know my job was
demanding...and I needed a few drinks after
work...to unwind.   And I've <u>always</u> played
golf with my friends on Saturdays...for fifteen years...it's been a tradition!   <u>Was</u> there
someone else?

2 miles to
THE WINDOW--
See the answer to any problem

I didn't expect I would feel so empty inside...so confused...so scared. What about
this new job? What if I can't turn the company around? What if I fail? If I don't make
a success of this a lot of people will be out
of work. Can I do it?

Turn here
THE WINDOW--
See the answer to any problem

Suddenly I jerked the steering wheel to
the right. It is probably just a scam of
some sort, but what the heck...I'm here...and
after six hours of driving I deserve a break.
I had gone about a half mile when I saw
the parking lot. It was filled to capacity!
There were huge semis, Winnebagos, expensive
sports cars, even battered station wagons--
every imaginable type of vehicle. There was
even a small fleet of motorcycles. The long
line of people waiting to enter a small,
shabby building was just as diverse as the
vehicles they came in. Each person seemed

intense.   Could this "window" actually re-
veal the answer to *any* problem--especially
one as complicated as *mine*?

The line seemed to move quickly so I didn't
mind the wait. Suddenly I noticed something
peculiar. There was a line of people who were
leaving the building. I studied their faces
to get some clue as what was waiting for me
at the "window".   The reactions were as var-
ied as the people themselves. Some were cry-
ing. Some were laughing. Some were embrac-
ing. Some looked stunned. One especially
well dressed woman, perhaps in her early for-
ties, was angry. She was shrieking that it
was a fraud. She was threatening to sue the
person who was responsible for this outrage.
None of the others seemed to be paying much
attention to her, and eventually she left--in
one of the expensive sports cars.

Soon I was inside the building. It was
dimly lit, and in the center of the room, near
the wall, was what appeared to be a small cubicle with a curtain across the front. Each
person stood in front of the cubicle as the
curtain was opened briefly--for maybe ten seconds. Just long enough for a quick glimpse
at the "window". As the curtain closed each

person turned and walked slowly to the door at the other end of the building.

When my turn came I stepped in front of the curtain. I must admit I was filled with anticipation. What was the answer to my problems? As I waited for the curtain to open the seconds seemed like hours. Suddenly it opened and instantly I realized the answer to my problems...and the key to my future, as well!

You see it wasn't a window, after all...**it was a <u>mirror</u>!**

I hurriedly left the building. I fumbled in my pocket for some coins. There must be a phone around here somewhere. Maybe I can catch Marsha before she leaves for work!

Heading home

It had been a long and very productive day, but at last I was heading home. It had seemed like a special day--a day when the 'earth spirits' had been active. Strange and unusual occurrences seemed to take place all day long. I can't explain these days, I only know they are days when a person needs to pay particular attention to everything that happens, because hidden messages and life lessons are everywhere. But now I was going home. The road was free of traffic. I was alone with my thoughts. I enjoy this kind of driving more and more.

I hadn't driven far when I thought I heard voices. I checked the radio. It was turned off. The voice seemed to get clearer, as if it were close at hand. It seemed strange, almost inhuman. For some reason my mind went to a speaker I had heard a few weeks earlier. She said she believed that animals had

a special gift for communicating over great
distances--especially at night. I hadn't
given the idea much thought. But now...a voice
was rattling around in my mind. The voice
was much clearer now and I could hear every
word...

*"I am heading home to you my beloved one.
Oh how I have missed you and our yearling.
But the separation was worth it. I have discovered the perfect home for us. There is
a valley--a very special valley--only a few
days away. Sweet green grasses are everywhere
and tender leaves hang low from the branches
of the trees. The bushes are heavy with ber-
ries. A clear, cool stream runs the length
of the valley. The cliffs surrounding the
valley will offer protection from the cold
winds and shade during the hot summer days.
At night cool breezes blow and the heavens
are filled with stars. It is so quiet and se-
rene. What did you say? Oh yes, I saw many
of our kind there. There were also bison,
antelope, elk, and some horses and cattle.
Even coyotes, bear, and wolves live there.
But everyone lives in harmony. We talked
as friends talk. We even laughed together.
There is no fear or anger in this valley...it*

is the place we have dreamed about. That is why I am coming home as fast as I can. After I cross this wide human road I will only be a few hours away from you. I am almost across. Suddenly I see bright lights. They blind my eyes! I can no longer see..."

I heard a dull thud and the voice was silent. About a mile ahead I could see a truck parked just off the road. I slowed down and as I got closer I saw the driver was pulling a deer carcass to the shoulder of the highway. I stopped to offer my help, but as I got out of my car I could see the driver had already removed the animal from the highway. The driver was kneeling beside the animal with his hat in his hand. As I approached I could see his eyes were closed and his lips were moving silently. He was praying! I stood in silence until he rose to his feet. Without taking his eyes from the deer he said softly. "Folks say they are dumb animals...I dunno. I figure they are God's creatures, just like you and me. I believe they have feelings and sensitivities, too--and families--just like us. I sure didn't mean to kill him."

He looked at me for the first time. "I was heading home. I had been away all week and I was in a hurry to see my wife and kids. Maybe

I had driven more than I should have today. Maybe I was going a little too fast…I dunno. I just came around the bend and there he was. I tried to stop…"

The tears in his eyes seemed somehow out of place for a man his size. "I called the highway patrol. They should be here soon." He looked at me for a moment. "You can go on home, if you like. I'm gonna' stay here awhile longer." He smiled slightly. "You drive careful now…you hear?"

"I will…I will."

I shook his hand and walked slowly back to my car. It was late, but the 'earth spirits' were still at work.

Living with Illusion

For some time I have been mulling over the concept of 'illusions' and how they affect our lives. What are 'illusions'? Are they good for us, or harmful? When in doubt I refer to my battered old dictionary. Mr. Webster says:

"Illusion—something that deceives the eye or mind; a mistaken perception or belief."

Webster appears to be saying that 'illusion' is not a good thing…a deceiver. And thus, living with illusion would appear to be a life based upon mistaken perceptions and erroneous beliefs. And yet illusions are all around us…many people base their entire lives upon one illusion or another. Oscar Wilde seemed to defend illusions when he wrote:

"The one person who has more illusions than the dreamer is the man of action."

How we react to our illusions will determine our outcomes. We can dwell on our perceptions and beliefs, mistaken and erroneous as they may be, and let an entire lifetime passes us by...or we can challenge our beliefs and in the end, do something with them. Someone once wrote:

"Pleasure can be supported by an illusion, but happiness rests upon truth."

Some people prefer their illusions and have no desire to put forth any effort to dispel them...even if they might suspect they are based upon misconceptions. In these instances they will never have the opportunity to experience the reality of life. Remember when Joni Mitchell sang:

**"I've looked at life from both sides now,
From win and lose and still somehow,
It's life's illusions I recall,
I really don't know life at all."**

It is life's illusions, our mistaken perceptions, that we often prefer to remember, rather than life's truths. Perhaps to some people it is easier to live with illusions than it is to challenge them and live with the truth.

Cyril Connolly supports this approach by saying:

"We must select the illusion which appeals to our temperament and embrace it with passion, if we want to be happy."

Some folks embrace memories from their past with a passion. They live their lives based upon events of the past. I am always amazed when I encounter a person in their 50s, 60s, and beyond who see their high school prom, or winning a particular ballgame as a teenager, as the highlight of their life. They seem to have lived an entire lifetime with nothing--no more significant achievements--no more memorable events to eclipse that dance or ballgame.

Equally amazing are the people who let their entire lifetime slip past as they eagerly anticipate some event that will surely take place in the not too distant future.

They are convinced that when they receive that particular promotion, or meet that special someone, or win the lottery, every one of their problems will instantly and miraculously disappear, and total ecstasy will be theirs for ever and ever. The fallacy is that when you live in the past, or in the expectations of the future, you are wasting valuable time. Your life is going to be over before you know it and you will have missed many of the joys and excitement connected with confronting reality. Consider this:

"I have realized that the past and future are real illusions, that they do not exist in the present which is what there is and all there is."

Alan Watts

I think this is an excellent way to approach life's illusions. Consider them-- savor them, if you must--but move on to the realities. That is really what life is all about--growth and successful living are getting beyond life's illusions and dealing with realities. I think it is best summarized by my friend Gurudevi Amalya Running Deer Mahakali, in her book <u>Clear Water</u>:

"So when things are not working for you, simply remember that you are not who you think you are, that you are more than you know and that all thoughts, challenges, problems, issues are nothing more than illusion."

You are more than you can possibly imagine. You have more talents, more skill, more intellect, than you realize to identify your 'illusions', confront them head-on, and to resolve them successfully. Live in the moment...today can be the best day of your life.

When it doesn't pay to be Mr. Nice Guy

There was a time a few years ago when we lived in a four-story townhouse in Alexandria, Virginia. One summer a family of sparrows built a nest in the outside vent for our clothes dryer. The vent was about ten feet above the ground with a sheer drop to the ground. In a few short months I noticed two tiny heads poking out of the shaggy makeshift nest. I wondered how in the world they would be able to grow and learn to fly in such cramped quarters. A few months later I got my answer. As I was raking the leaves from around the bushes below the vent I discovered two tiny dead baby birds.

I admit I was a bit upset at the time. I blamed the parents for not building their nest in a more appropriate site…such as in a tree or in a the shelter of a dormer. And then I forgot about the incident. Okay, I thought about it once in awhile. But I didn't obsess about it.

The following spring I did get a bit upset when I noticed a new nest had been built in the vent. Hadn't they learned their lesson last year? Didn't they care that the previous year's brood had perished before they ever had a chance at life? What were they thinking? I figured enough is enough. I got my ladder out and pulled the nest from the vent. It was two good-sized handfuls of matted twigs, string, and leaves. I threw the nest into the gutter beside the curb and went out to run a few errands.

When I returned an hour later I noticed some debris protruding from the vent. Again I got my ladder out and climbed to check it out. In the time I was gone Mr. Sparrow had rebuilt the nest! He had somehow managed to get that considerable pile of stuff back into the vent! I couldn't help but feel this bird might be very industrious, but he sure wasn't the brightest candle on the cake. Again I removed the new nest. This time I threw the material down a storm drain. I figured that was the end of it. But as I sat down just below the vent I realized Mr. Sparrow was

watching me from behind the trunk of a neighbor's tree. From time to time he would peek
around the trunk and loudly scold me. When I
went over to the front of the tree he would
hop to a branch at the back of the tree. For
a time we played a little game of cat and
mouse. After a time he flew away and I returned to my chair. Within minutes a small
piece of paper drifted down from the vent.
I looked up and lo and behold, Mrs. Sparrow
was still inside the vent. I had had it! I
chased her from the vent and closed it with
a broomstick. I was sure that would be the
end of it.

But within minutes she was back. She flew
to the top of the tree just in front of the
vent and began to scold me. After a few moments she flew across the street to another
tree. I could still hear her shrieking at
me. Then she flew back to our tree and scold-
ed me some more. For the next half-hour she
repeated the process. Back and forth across
the street…each time she returned she landed
on lower branch until she was just above my
head.

If birds can swear I am certain she tossed
every profanity she knew in my direction. I
tried to explain that I only destroyed their

nest to prevent the potential death of her unborn babies. She didn't seem to care about my motives. To her I was the nasty guy who destroyed her home. All this time her hen-pecked spouse hid in the tree next door. He continued to shriek at me, but he didn't have the guts to do it to my face.

To put an end to this charade I finally said, as plain as I could, that I was only concerned for the little ones. I further promised that if they decided to rebuild the nest I would not disturb it.

...and they did!

The Gift of Appreciative Living

One of the greatest gifts we can give ourselves is the gift of Appreciative Living. Essentially Appreciative Living is the ability to recognize the best in yourself, the people around you, and in your current circumstances. This is not a matter of looking through the proverbial rose-colored glasses and seeing only the positive aspects of everything. That is a bit unrealistic even in the best of times. Appreciative Living is much, much more.

It is the ability to live in the moment and to <u>recognize</u> and <u>extract</u> the best of that moment. It is not easy. In fact it can be pretty complicated at times.

An important aspect of this gift is the ability to recognize and experience the abundance of life. You see, we often spend too much time trying to <u>have</u> what we <u>want</u>...rather than <u>wanting</u> what we already <u>have</u>. You

may say, "What can I do? I have no money!"
or "What can I do? I have an affliction or
handicap?" or "I have problems with an ad-
diction."

Really?

Look at many of the great artists--writers,
painters, poets, and leaders--that struggled
with these same issues. Yet, within them were
great works of art. Helen Keller was born
blind and deaf…and she became one of the most
outstanding women of the 20th Century. Franklin Delano Roosevelt was crippled with polio,
and he was elected to a fourth term as President of the United States.

In my opinion, the principal authority and
proponent on the subject of Appreciative Living was Dr. Donald C. Klein, author of **"New
Reality, New Vision"**. Dr. Klein wrote:

**"Our initial commitment to Appreciative
Living sets in process a wonderful cycle: the
more negatives we release, the more energy we
have available for living; the more energy
we have available, the more Appreciative we
become of the delight and wonder of everyday
life; the more Appreciative we allow ourselves
to be, the more energy we find at our disposal.
On and on and on in an ever-increasing cycle,**

Appreciating generates an evermore expansive awareness of what it means to be alive.

What a delightful philosophy for living to use as a basis for living a full, rich life. Dr. Klein goes on to say:

"As any adult who has ever watched a child at play knows, Appreciation—simple and child-like as it is—is a powerful and intensely illuminating way to experience life. With Appreciation comes a variety of gifts, subjects that have fascinated sages, philosophers, and religious leaders throughout the ages."

Dr. Klein suggests four 'gifts' that form the foundation of Appreciative Living:

Clarity: an intensity, brightness, and vividness that make even the familiar and time-worn seem brand-new.

To be able to see your personal circumstances and the problems around you clearly and with a greater insight is in itself a special gift. You not only benefit from a better understanding of the complete problem, but you also gain a better insight into

the options you have at your disposal to use
to remedy the situation. You are able to
recognize the various ways you can use to resolve the problem once and for all.

**<u>Joy</u>: a collection of positive feelings of
wonder, ecstasy, and delight in life; a sense
that "all is well".**

This means being able to face each day with
a positive sense that things will work out in
time, a sense of knowing that basically life
is good, that you have a right to the pursuit
of happiness. (That is, as long as you seek
it through legal and non-violent means, as
long as you don't tromp on other people in
the process.) When you learn to appreciate
'life', and work toward giving joy, rather
than merely seeking to receive it, you will
quickly recognize how much of it there is to
go around. And the more people who recognize
the importance and significance of 'appreciative living' the more the spirit of joy and
happiness will grow and multiply.

In her wonderful book **Excuse Me, Your Life
is Waiting**, Lynn Grabhorn wrote:

"When you are in Joy with Life you cannot vibrate negatively and you cannot _attract_ negatively, only positively."

Joy is important because it allows us to not only experience life, but to better un-derstand it...to take our full share of it...to fully appreciate it...to fully value it. Life is important! Living life with a heightened sense of Joy allows us to give...and to take! We have a right...a Divine right, if you will, to love Life and to appreciate it completely. To do this we must live each day completely. This necessitates that we experience Joy each day of our lives.

You may say, "Whoa there...how can I have joy in my life if I'm concerned about my finances, my health, my relationships, my job, etc." When you have a sense of Joy about your Life you are able to realize that all these things are really just temporary. You can rise above any of these issues if you can accept the fact that in time all problems can, and will be resolved. Think about that for a mo-ment. One of my favorite verses in the Bible is found in Saint Paul's letter to the people of Philippi. He was in prison, facing death when he wrote:

**"I know both how to be abased, and I know
how to abound; every where and in all things
I am instructed both to be full and to be
hungry, both to abound and to suffer need."**

Philippians 4:12 KJV

I can relate to this scripture. I have
experienced many highs and lows in my lifetime. I have experienced tremendous turmoil
and sadness…even deep depression at times.
I have also experienced jubilant highs that
bordered upon pure euphoria. In all honesty
I can not pinpoint the precise moment all
this changed. But it did, and I have been
able to experience a sense of Joy on some
level each day…every day. I like to think
that scripture has helped. But the point I
want to make is that if you allow a sense of
Joy to be a part of your daily life, Appreciative Living becomes more natural and you
can live a more productive, more bountiful
Life. And that's a promise!

**Creativity: a sure intuitive grasp of sit-
uations, a 'knowingness' that allows us to
cut through complexity to see immediately
what needs to be done.**

It is difficult for me to think about 'creativity' without thinking about Michaelangelo. He often said that he was able to recognize the 'spirit' of his subjects in the blocks of marble...and that he merely cut away the stone until that 'spirit' was released. Creativity as experienced through Appreciative Living is just that. The Gift provides the ability to look at a problem or issue and see what must be done to resolve it. It allows us to sift through the chaff to get to the heart of the problem and to resolve it. The Gift, as Michaelangelo put it, helps us to release the 'spirit' of the problem or issue and get on with our lives.

Energy: vitality, a strong sense of emotional well-being, an absence of stress that allows us to focus our mental, physical, and emotional resources on whatever task or situation lies immediately before us.

When we learn to appreciate life we have more energy to focus all of our resources on the problems and issues that prevent us from living full, rich lives. As Dr. Klein points out, the more negatives we are able to release, the more energy we have to experience the positive aspects of life.

I met a woman a few months ago who put this all in perspective for me. She has been confined to a wheelchair for over a decade, and yet she continues to teach four classes each day at an inner-city high school. In addition she teaches English two nights a week to classes of immigrants from over two dozen foreign countries. She spends several hours each week teaching life skills to other people confined to wheelchairs. Oh, she is also writing a book. When I asked her how she found the energy to keep up with her demanding schedule she smiled and said simply, "I really appreciate my life!"

I believe in that single sentence she has best summarized the true value of the Gift of Appreciative Living.

Water, water everywhere, but...

We are all familiar with this old line. But it draws our attention to several major problems that lie just ahead of us all. We take water for granted. We turn on the spigot and out flows water. We take a drink, wash our hands, wash our car, water our plants. No problem.

Well guess what, folks. In some areas it is a problem, and one that gets more serious with each passing year. Now, I'm not an alarmist. I don't believe the sky is falling. I tend to believe that all problems will eventually be resolved when good people become concerned enough to act responsibly and take action.

But this water thing is a horse of a different color. People--a large number of people--see water as an entitlement. They view water as a commodity, something that will always be available and abundant. They refuse to consider that the supply of water is finite. They see the ocean...or the Great Lakes...or even a stream after a spring rain, and they laugh, "How could water be in short supply?" Every year a river floods and people's homes are washed away. Sometimes entire communities are affected. A hurricane or typhoon hits an area with high winds and torrential down-pours. A large area is completely destroyed. You look at the headlines and the newscasts and say, "Whadda you mean there is a short-age of water? Look at that mess!" But you don't often stop to think that more and more of our existing supply of potable water...that is unpolluted and untainted water...is disap-pearing at an ever-increasing rate.

My concern really began to grow when I visited a glacier in Canada and saw how far that mass of ice had receded in a fraction of my lifetime. I must say it was an eye opening experience. After moving to Arizona I became even more concerned when we drove up to Lake Mead and saw that the water level was far below what it once was. To make matters worse the experts say that statistical models indicate it will never be full again. In addition, the Colorado River, which feeds Lake Mead is at its lowest level since measurements, began some 85 years ago. Seven states, including Colorado, Utah, Wyoming, New Mexico, Arizona, California, and Nevada depend on the Colorado for all or part of their water needs. To make matters worse this is one of the fastest growing areas in the nation. And many of the new comers fail to see that living in a desert limits their ability to have big lawns and flower gardens.

Some experts believe a city should have a five-year supply of water in reserve. I'm not certain how practical this is, but I do believe we have to think about some creative ways to conserve our most necessary resource, before we face a greater crisis.

There is also an economic consideration. Economic growth throughout the nation is dependent on having a constant supply of water. In the state of Colorado alone the agricultural community uses as much as 90% of the water. If we can't produce the food we need to feed our nation, or provide jobs for our people, we are in a serious situation. But even the early settlers were concerned over the amount of water available in the west. Many reported back to our leaders in the east that this area was inhospitable because of a lack of water. For years our leaders have expressed concern over the possibility of water shortages. Back in 1955, over 50 years ago, Ezra Taft Benson, the U.S. Secretary of Agriculture wrote:

"I have little need to remind you that water has become one of our major national concerns."

Gil Stern has hit the nail on the head:

"Man is a complex being: he makes deserts bloom and lakes die."

Somehow, at least to this point, we have been able to stretch the available water to support an ever-growing number of families and industries, but we all have to be prepared to make changes in our life styles in the months and years to come if we are to leave a legacy of ample water for future generations.

And there is a related problem that should also get our attention. That is the problem brought about because of bottled water. When I lived in New York I was amazed at the number of people who carried a bottle of water with them everywhere they went. And I mean everywhere! They carried them to work, on the subway, while they shopped, even as they ate in restaurants. And of course some of the discarded bottles actually made it into trashcans…many did not. Not only do these discards litter our city streets, but also millions upon millions of them are found in our parks, along highways, and even along our hiking trails. Is nothing sacred? Some people who worry about secondhand smoke, global warming, and the disappearing rain forest, will think nothing of discarding an empty water bottle. Even those thoughtful folks who dispose of the bottles in trashcans are part of a growing problem. The discards end up in landfills where they will languish for decades before they disappear completely.

Think about that for a moment. This is a huge industry…billions of bottles are produced and sold each week. (I could add the billions of bottles of soft drinks that are sold and disposed of each day…but at the moment I am thinking about the water issue.) Relatively few bottle carcasses are recycled. If that weren't enough…these bottles are *plastic*…they are petroleum-based…it takes many, many gallons of precious oil to produce them! At a time when everyone is concerned over our nation's extravagant use of oil, few people think about this area of consumption.

By all means drink plenty of water. It is good for you. Experts tell us eight glasses a day are essential for good health. If portability is important, the purchase of a reusable water container could help solve several problems. But if you must drink purchased, bottled water be mindful of the importance of recycling. Oh, and you might want to think about this…much of what is sold bottled is plain, ordinary tap water. C'mon folks, you didn't really think it was from a pristine, virgin waterfall in some remote area, did you?

But getting back to the concern over water conservation. If we run out of water the other concerns are moot, aren't they? The question we all should consider is this. As citizens of the world, how do we assume our responsibility to conserve and protect the water that is essential to the future of our planet?

President John F. Kennedy summed the water issue rather succinctly when he wrote:

"Anyone who can solve the problems of water will be worthy of two Nobel prizes—one for peace and one for science"

A Bundle of Possibilities

A few years ago I was living in New York City and taking one of many, many subway rides. Across the aisle from me was a young mother with her two children. One of the girls was sitting in a stroller. She had an unruly mop of curls, a big smile, and a boisterous laugh. Everyone who passed by patted her head and commented to her mother about how cute she was. The mother beamed and thanked each person for his or her kind words.

Seated next to the young mother was another daughter. I would guess she was nine or ten years of age. By contrast, no one was paying any attention her. She was sitting quietly with her head down. For some time I watched the little girl. That sad little face touched me. Then a strange thing happened. I felt a sudden urge to speak to the little girl and offer some words of encouragement.

I dismissed the urge as ridiculous. This is New York! Who would dare to approach a young girl on a subway...even if her mother was sitting beside her? Still the urge persisted. No way! There was no way I would have the nerve to speak to a strange child. Most of the time I don't speak to strange adults unless they speak to me first. But the urging continued to increase in intensity.

As my stop approached I stood up. Suddenly I was speaking to her. "Are you good in school?" I asked. She looked up shyly. "Uh huh." Then suddenly the following words spilled out of my mouth. "You need to work real hard, because someday you are going to do something special!"

I walked quickly to the door. But before I exited I turned and looked again at the little girl. Her mother had turned to her and was speaking softly. "Did you hear that man? You need to work hard...because you are *special*!" The little girl nodded and smiled proudly. She was positively glowing.

I left the train in shock. My heart was pounding and I was perspiring heavily. What had just happened? I had no idea. Even as I sit here, separated from the incident by several years and thousands of miles, I am still in awe. I still don't believe those were my words! I was merely a conduit through which a higher power spoke to a little girl some words she needed to hear. But why me? Why that particular moment in time? Why not in a dream? Why did the words not come from a parent or a close relative? Why not from a teacher…her minister? I will never know the answer. I only know that for some reason I was used at that point in time to pass that important message on to that little girl.

I will never see her again. I will never know the impact those words had, or will have, as her life unfolds. I can only know that I was a small part of something that was supposed to happen. If I had ignored the urging, if I had not spoken to the girl, that *something* may not have taken place. But I am equally certain, however, that if I had not responded to the urging, the power behind it would have found another to get the message to her.

I share this experience with you in the hope that if you are ever in that position, if you are being urged to offer a message of encouragement or support to a perfect stranger that you give it a great deal of thought before you dismiss it and walk on.

Shank's Mare

For some reason the term 'Shank's Mare' has been spinning around in my head for the past several weeks. That is usually an indication that I need to sit down and write about it. I tried to think about where I had heard the term, and why it was tucked away in my memory bank. I attribute it to my Grandfather Armstrong. He was a man of few words, having spent many of his formative years in an orphanage or being passed from one foster family to another. His education had been meager. In those days orphans and children of the poor went to work early in life. School was a luxury few could afford. But even with his limited education he would, on occasion, use a phrase that to my ears would border on the obscure. To the best of my recollection he would say something like, "I got there by *Shank's mare.*" Or, "The only way to get there was by *Shank's mare.*"

As a child I always assumed that on those occasions a generous neighbor by the name of Shank had loaned him a horse. But recently a little research clarified it for me. You see, my grandfather was of Scottish decent... several generations removed, but Scottish none the less. And the term Shank's mare had its origin in Scotland.

To quote Michael Quinion from World Wide Words:

It's Scottish, dating from the eighteenth century. There was a verb, to *shank* or to *shank it*, meaning to go on foot. This is from Standard English *shank* for the part of the leg from the knee to the ankle, which comes from Old English *sceanca*, the leg bone. This verb developed into *shank's naig* or *shank's naigie* (where the second words are local forms of *nag*, a horse) and later into *shank's mare*. It was a wry joke: I haven't got a horse of my own for the journey, so I'll use Shank's mare to get there, meaning I'll go on my own two feet. This supposed link with a person called Shank explains why the first word is often capitalized.

So with all this in mind I have been trying to figure out why, all of a sudden, this
phrase has been racing through my mind.   I
mean it isn't like we travel much by Shank's
mare in this day and age.   Most of us just
jump into our cars for even short excursions.
I admit I drive to the trailheads that lead
to my favorite writing spots.   Though without
Shank's mare I could never get to the most
secluded of those retreats.

But beyond that I was thinking about one of
my favorite subjects of late...our Earth Walk.
While the term 'Earth Walk' is symbolic of
our life's journey, I think that the walking
part...Shank's mare, if you will...is an important part of the journey.   When walking we
are able to take in and to better appreciate
our surroundings, to see up close the rich
tapestry of color in the changing of the sea-
sons, the waking of the Earth at dawn, the
rich sunsets at the close of the day, the many
subtle changes that make up each new day.

Too often, as we rush through each day,
we miss these special moments.   Our children grow up and leave home.   Our neighbors
and co-workers come and go without our even
taking the time to share our blessings with

them, or partaking of the wisdom and knowledge they have to share with us.

What a pity! We rush through our lives so quickly that we spend precious little time enriching and being enriched by those around us. I guess the moral here is that we need to slow down a bit and take the time to smell the roses.

We all need to be intentional about our Earth Walk--to seek out our life's Purpose. But at the same time we need to travel at a pace that allows us to drink in the rich ambiance that is all around us. Maybe we should rely more on Shank's mare to set the pace for our Earth Walk. Maybe we should slow down a bit so we can better enjoy all the rich experiences that await us along the journey.

I guess this brings me full circle to thoughts of Grandpa Armstrong. I can still see him under the big maple tree…sitting in his homemade wooden chair, and smoking his old corncob pipe. He only smoked 5 Brothers tobacco. He usually had a slight smile. I always thought of it as a look of complete satisfaction. It was the satisfied smile of a man who knew he had been dealt a difficult hand but he had played that hand to the best

of his ability. Maybe his journey on Shank's
mare--his Earth Walk--had taken him where he
needed to go.

Prime the Pump

Years ago a popular singing group known as The Kingston Trio recorded a song entitled "Desert Pete". In essence the song tells a story about a man lost in the desert. He is near death when he happens upon an old rusty pump. On the pump he finds a note that tells him that the pump is in good working order and that if he will only take the bottle of water hidden under a nearby rock and use it to prime the pump he will be spared.

According to the note the traveler should prime the pump by taking this bottle of precious life saving water and pouring it into the top of the pump. Then, by pumping the handle up and down vigorously, he would get enough water to fill his needs. The note continues...

"Drink all the water you can hold, wash your face, cool your feet. *But leave the bottle full for others*.

Thank you kindly, Desert Pete

Therein lies a conflict of sorts. The dying man knows he can take the bottle of water he has in his hand and by carefully rationing it he can reach safety. But what about the next person who comes to the pump in need of water? How will they survive if there is no bottle of water with which to prime the pump? Should he take the water and use it only to address his immediate needs, or should he also be concerned about the needs of those who follow in his footsteps? It is a matter of responsibility. What would you do? Would you take the water for yourself--or prime the pump and leave a bottle for others?

The message ol' Desert Pete is trying to get across is simply this—there is an abundance of everything available to us, but we should only take enough to supply our needs and make certain there is a sufficient amount for those who come after us.

This message is relevant for many areas—there is plenty of money, food, love and affection, fame, etc.—more than enough for

everyone. The problem is that it is often
concentrated in one area when the need is
someplace else. As caring human beings it is
our role...our duty...to help spread it around—to
get it to where it can do the most good.

Interestingly enough there is a law called
"The Law of Attraction". This law says simply that we get what we think about. In
other words, if you think about blessings
they will be attracted to you. If you let
your thoughts dwell upon on pain and hard-
ships they will be drawn to you. This may
sound harsh on some level, but I believe the
law is true. I have seen it in my own life.
But even though it is true in most lives, it
is difficult to make believers out of most
people. Someone wrote:

**We do not always get what we WANT, or even
what we feel we NEED, but we always get what
we EXPECT!**

Desert Pete is pointing out that we need
to 'ante up'...to make the first move. Most
often it is probably to perform some unself-
ish act of kindness...to do something special
for another person without any expectation of
something in return. Ideally this is the way

we should live. But all too often we hesi-
tate until we can evaluate the cost of the
action to us personally. "Is this going to
take too much of my money?" "Is it going to
require too much of my time?" "What is in
it for me?"

When you can respond to the needs of others
from the heart…automatically, abundance will
begin to flow in your direction. This doesn't
mean that by performing acts of kindness you
are going to suddenly become rich! At least
in monetary terms…your wealth will probably
be measured with different yardsticks.

Douglas K. Freeman summed it up with these
words:

**"If you want to know the value of an in-
dividual, ask not for the sum of all that he
owns, but look instead to the total of all
that he has given."**

I think ol' Desert Pete would be happy if
we would all take this to heart.

Kachina Woman

From my first visit to Sedona I developed a strange attraction to the Kachina Woman, a towering rock formation that stands a few hundred yard off the trail to Boynton Canyon. When I moved to the Sedona area my first hike was to the foot of that majestic landmark. I sat for several hours looking up at her from every angle. I don't know exactly what I expected, but I left feeling I had missed something. For the next several weeks I thought on any number of occasions about this symbol with such strong ties to the native people. I made another pilgrimage up the trail, and again I sat for several hours meditating. Once more I left with that strange empty sensation...that something important had escaped my grasp.

For the next week or so the "lady" became almost an obsession. I thought a great deal about her 'story'. What secrets had she held for all these years? Or was I completely off base? Was she in reality just what she appeared to be…a large rock formation that bore some slight resemblance to a female body?

On my third visit I did something that I understand has been part of some tribal traditions. I carried with me a small pouch filled with ground corn. As I walked slowly around the 'lady' I scattered a portion of the ground corn at her feet. As I walked I prayed for wisdom and insight. I do this in the hope that the words I write or speak will be of some significance to those who hear or read them. When I had exhausted my tribute I sat down on a rock and looked up at her.

"What is it that draws me here? Why do you hold such a fascination for me? Do you have some wisdom that would help me help others?"

For a brief moment the ground seemed to tremble. A mist, or maybe it was a low flying cloud, seemed to encircle the top of the rock formation. In a low whisper she spoke to me, "You have been persistent, my son, and you have taken the time to learn of customs of my people. But I do not believe I possess any special knowledge or wisdom that will be of benefit to you in your Earth Walk."

I was dumbfounded. After a few moments I was able to stammer, "You seem to have something that draws me to you like a magnetic force. I can't explain it, but that is how it feels."

"I am just a spirit that loves this special land and the native people. For centuries I have watched over them and tried to help them." There was a slight pause.

"But, no meaningful wisdom is the special possession of any one person. It is in the flowing waters, and on the lips of all creatures, great and small. True wisdom travels on the wind to the four corners of the Earth. It is available to any person who takes the time to absorb it and use it to achieve good works."

"So then, you are like a God to the native people?"

"Oh my no...Earth Mother nurtures all people. At the same time each people has a special spirit guide to watch over them. From the time they first came to this land I have been with them...to guide and protect them."

For a few moments there was silence. Then she spoke. "You have a question, my son?"

I hesitated. "Yes, but I'm not sure it is appropriate to ask it of you."

She smiled and spoke softly, "I have looked into your heart and I know you mean well. What is your question?"

"I have seen many 'Kachina dolls' for sale in the stores…some even appear to be fierce in appearance. Which one most truly represents you?"

"All of them." She paused for a moment. "You see, my spirit is in the planter of seeds as it is in the one who harvests the crops. My spirit is in the warrior when enemies attack my people. My spirit is also in the peacemaker, in the shaman who heals the sick, in the women who bear children, and in the teachers who educate them. My spirit dwells within every native person who lives his or her life with a reverence for the Earth Mother. I even dwell in the hearts of those that have finished their Earth Walk and have joined their ancestors."

She paused and looked at me with a gentle, but intense gaze. "Many years ago the Earth Mother sought to give me a reward for my service. She offered me the opportunity to live for all eternity with her in the world beyond the sky. I chose instead to come here…to remain in this place where I could continue to look after my beloved people. And so it has been for many years. To me this was the best possible reward."

I noticed the sun was setting and her image was beginning to grow a bit dim. "May I come again to talk with you?" I asked.

"I don't believe so. If you wish to meditate over an issue that could benefit my people, come to this place and I will try to give you guidance. I will always speak in the spirit to any person who comes here pure of heart, and with a sincere desire to help my people. But I can not again speak with you. So go now, and continue your journey in peace."

As she spoke these words the earth trembled slightly and the Kachina Woman again took her place as the silent sentinel overlooking the land of her beloved people. I sat in silence for a few moments carefully considering her words. Then I arose and walked slowly back down the mountain. The emptiness I had experienced on previous visits was gone. There was a sense of renewal in my spirit. I felt an enthusiasm for the future and the challenges that awaited me in the days ahead.

Nevertheless...

It is strange how a word or phrase jumps into your mind and caroms around and around like the steel ball in a pinball machine. You wonder where it came from? Why does it seem to adhere to your every thought for a time, and then just disappear again into the remote recesses of your subconscious? Today, for some strange reason, the phrase 'nevertheless' is bouncing around in my brain. It isn't an unfamiliar or foreign phrase to me; I use it from time to time. But it got me thinking about the context in which we might find ourselves using the word. It is a great word for people engaged in debating an issue, or people who are objecting to one thing or another. I'm sure politicians are the most frequent users of the word. They seem to spend most of their time debating and/or objecting.

It is a great term to use after you have made a concession, but still have a point or two you feel is worthy of further consideration.

"John certainly has his faults, nevertheless he has worked tirelessly to overcome his anger issues."

It is also useful when you want to show there is a point worthy of adding to your own conclusions.

"Yes we do need to stomp out terrorism, nevertheless we should avoid harming innocent people...particularly innocent women and children."

It is also useful when you want to make the other person realize how much you value their input, as in:

"Nevertheless, I can understand your point of view and will certainly consider it when making my decision".

I was in the middle of presenting a Pathways to PURPOSE workshop awhile back when a rather elderly man put up his hand to ask a question. His question left me at a loss for words. He asked, "How can a 'loving' God take the life of a teenager who has his whole life ahead of him?" Since my workshops are 'spiritual' by nature as opposed to being a 'religious' program, the question threw me for a moment. It had little if anything to do with what I had been talking about. Before I could gather my wits and attempt a response he continued. "Years ago, when I had my scout troop, one of my boys drowned while we were at a campout. He was a good boy...one of the best in my troop. He never did anything bad in his whole life. He was a good student. He took care of his younger brothers and sisters while his mother was at work. He went to church every Sunday. He was a good boy...he didn't deserve to die!"

He became increasingly emotional as he spoke. I noticed his wife reached over and took his hand in hers. Her eyes filled with tears. I suddenly realized that he was talking about something that had taken place in the far distant past, but was still troubling him--deeply troubling him. I had been talking about how we often need to look beyond an experience to find a hidden lesson that can help lead us to our life's Purpose. Apparently something in that concept had opened an old wound that even his wife believed had healed. I wondered how long that man had grieved in silence over that incident. Perhaps his grief had remained intact even though the boy's own family had grieved and moved on with their lives.

As often happens in situations that require wisdom far greater than I possess, some words came from my lips that seemed to give him a measure of comfort. I have no idea what those words were, but I am always deeply appreciative of those moments when somehow the proper words seem to tumble forth at just the right time. I believe, on some level, it is the Creator helping me make up for some of the dumb and perhaps even hurtful words I have spoken in the past. Nevertheless...

I guess the primary reason for the term bouncing around in my mind so much at this particular time was a recent sermon given a few weeks back by my friend Dr. George A. Ault. Dr. Ault said:

"A good word for the last word, "Nevertheless". In a very real way that is what faith is all about. It takes an honest look at all the evil in the world. It faces all of life's confusions, its frustrations, its sufferings, its disasters, and says: "Nevertheless."

The Gift of 'Gifts'

In most of my presentations and workshops I make a point of referring to
these words of wisdom...

Yesterday is history,
Tomorrow is a mystery,
Today is a gift from God,
That is why it is called...
The PRESENT.

The point being, of course, that yesterday is over. The successes and failures of
yesterday are done. We can't change them.
They are past tense. And tomorrow is far
off in the distance. We shouldn't waste a
great deal of time worrying about what may
or may not happen. We can not be paralyzed
in anticipation of events we hope will occur
tomorrow. We can not quit our day jobs no
matter how sure we are that we will win the
lottery.

If we surrender to living in the past or thinking only about the future we will miss out on a great gift-- the gift of TODAY. The gift of a clean slate--a beautiful and pristine new day, and the opportunity to make of it what we choose. It is like a lump of moist clay awaiting the creative touch of a skilled artist.

But the 'gifts' I'm thinking about today are gifts of a different nature. They are the special tools we were each given at birth to help us achieve our life's PURPOSE.

You will be familiar with these 'gifts'. You have read about them and probably spent some time thinking about them. The problem is that most of us tend to think of them as gifts that are given to other people. We don't often think of them as they apply to our personal lives.

The first of these 'gifts' is the gift of **Intuition.** Webster defines 'intuition' as:

"Comprehension without effort of reasoning; instinctive knowledge".

I think of it as your internal guidance system. Your Intuition is infallible. It is truthful. It lays out the facts before you in clear, unemotional, non-judgmental language. It is then up to you to accept, or reject it. Anything you add to it to make it be more in line with your own wishes and desires will invalidate the value of the 'gift'.

The second 'gift' is **Synchronicity**. According to Webster, synchronicity is:

"The coincidental occurrence of events and especially psychic events that seem related but are not explained by conventional mechanisms of causality."

To me synchronicity is a connecting principle that manifests itself through one or more meaningful coincidence or events. That would include recurring events, dreams, and thoughts. If something seems to be happening to you with some regularity, pay careful attention to it. It could be an indication that it contains an important message for you.

Carl Jung spent years studying synchronicity. He concluded that true synchronicity is not related to cause and effect. We've been taught that everything is related to cause and effect. Do something good and you are rewarded. Do something bad and you are punished. But synchronicity does not work that way. A true synchronistic event will not be related to something you initiated. For instance, if you call a friend and leave a message, and the next day they call you when you are thinking about them, that is probably NOT synchronicity. You initiated the activity. But if you are thinking about someone you haven't seen in years and they suddenly send you a letter, or call you, that could be synchronistic because you did not initiate the event. In such cases you should carefully consider the impact of the event and what significance it could hold for you. Jung also concluded that synchronistic events are most likely to occur during emotional experiences and in times of transition. In each case a synchronistic event should be considered important and given a great deal of thought and consideration. It could be an indication of something important in your life's journey.

The third 'gift' is the gift of **Symbiosis**. Webster defines 'symbiosis' in part as:

"The close union of dissimilar organisms in a mutually beneficial relationship."

I prefer to think of 'symbiosis' as the **external flow of inspiration and direction.** It is the counterpart of intuition, which is the **internal** guidance system. There is an old saying,

"When the student is ready, the teacher will come."

Think of it this way. Whenever you are facing a crossroads in your life, and you need to make an important decision, someone will appear to help you--to provide advice, guidance, or direction. Leah Maggie Garfield wrote in her book, **Angels and Companions in Spirit**:

"None of us alone; it is not permitted...the Holy Spirit has a multitude of emissaries whom we refer to as 'guardian angels'. Many times a so-called guardian angel is in fact a lifetime guide."

As I have said these 'gifts' are for everyone and in abundance. The supply will never become exhausted. Take and use these special gifts as often as you have need of them.

Then there are the gifts you just know you
have to have--money, possessions, special
skills, a particular job, etc. You would do
anything to acquire them. You even try to
bargain with the Creator to have them.

I enjoy the story about the fellow who was
late for an appointment and needed a parking
place. He drove around for quite some time
with no success. Finally, in a fit of desper-
ation decided to pray about it. He prayed,
"Dear God, if you give me a parking place I
promise to attend church every Sunday. I
will give ten percent of all I possess to the
poor. I will never say anything mean about
anybody ever again." Just then a car pulled
out of a parking space just in front of the
building where he had the appointment. He
quickly pulled his car into the space. Then
he looked up and said, "Never mind, God, I
found one!"

Sometimes you feel your pleas have been
answered and you have actually received these
things you prayed to get. Although, in most
cases, if you are honest with yourself, you
will realize that you have these skills or
gifts because you worked tirelessly to acquire or develop them.

But in most cases the 'gifts' of greatest importance to you, the ones you need to pay the most attention to, are the gifts you **did not ask for**...the ones you didn't pray for...or plead for...or bargain for. The gifts I am referring to are the ones that just seem to appear out of the blue. You didn't ask for them. Maybe you don't even want them. But there they are, right before your eyes.

These gifts are of the greatest significance because in the Creator's mind...according to His Master Plan...you needed these gifts to better serve His needs. You may have prayed for the skills to be a good doctor...healing skills. But He gave you instead the gift of a great singing voice. You may, through your hard work and determination, become a great doctor. That is certainly to your credit. But do not ignore that gift of a singing voice. Find some way to use it. Maybe you don't give up your medical practice to become an opera singer, but you could certainly find time to sing in your church choir.

Lord only knows how often I've prayed to able to be able to hit long, straight drives on the golf course...how many hours I've spent on a driving range. But that skill continues to elude me. I didn't set out to be a writer.

I didn't ask for, or pray for, or seek out in any way the gift of putting words together. And yet it turns out that more people seem to benefit from the words He puts into my pen than will ever notice that one good drive I hit during each round of golf. I have to assume that is the way He wants it. Okay, I still work on my golf swing, but I will continue to faithfully write down the thoughts and ideas He puts into my heart.

Work faithfully to use each of the 'gifts' you have been given...those you asked for, and those you *did not ask for*. Each 'gift' is important, or it would not have been given to YOU!

A Scientific Analysis of the
Art of Waving

Okay, at best it a *semi*-scientific analysis. Each morning I walk for at least an hour. Part of my routine includes walking west on Cornville Road toward Cottonwood. As I walked I began to wave at the drivers of the cars and trucks headed toward Cornville. I began to notice certain patterns in the responses I received to my efforts. This led to the following collection of data. First of all…the wave itself. I find the most effective wave is the one I refer to as the "Five Finger Extended". Very simply, the FFE is the hand open with all five fingers extended, with the palm facing traffic. The arm is vertical to the elbow waist high. This wave receives a similar response from a full 87% of the oncoming traffic. By twisting the wrist from side to side you get a duplicate response from another 7% of the drivers.

It should be noted here that the Queen of England is famous for her use of a similar version of the FFE. However, in her version the hand twists in a slightly circular motion. Her version is much limper and not perceived as sincere as the FFE described above. The limp version receives little or no response from the drivers on the Cornville Road.

Another wave I have studied is the "FFF". It is essentially the same as the "FFE" except that it is dropped down laterally in a single motion to approximately 2 to 3 o'clock. It will receive a mirrored response in 3 to 5% of the time.

Now here is some other information for those of you who might be considering the Art of the Wave as a potential new hobby. First of all, if there are three vehicles in a row, the third driver will usually not respond to generic wave intended for all three vehicles. However, if you quickly close and reopen your hand it will usually be sufficient to get a return wave. If there are more than three vehicles in a row the responses drop off precipitously after the third one.

If you encounter a driver drinking coffee and talking on a cell phone cut off the wave immediately. They tend to be the most vigorous responders, and that is just down right dangerous. I have also noted that the passengers in these vehicles wave only at the rate of 31% of the time, unless they are construction workers. Passengers in construction vehicles wave 48% of the time.

School teachers, police officers, and senior women are the least responsive. They tend to keep both hands on the steering wheel and look straight ahead.

Responses also vary by season and time of day. As fall approaches and the angle of the sun changes responses will drop by as much as 16%. Remember that I am walking west and these drivers are facing the sun. When my shadow extends over 23 ½ feet, responses drop another 13%. I attribute that to visibility rather than to a lessening of friendliness.

In the end, the most important thing to remember is that the vast majority of the people are waving back! I like to think that everyone who waves back is getting his or her day off to a good start. So help me out…first thing tomorrow morning start waving at everyone you meet. Let's see if can't get something good started.

Anger

Anger is a strange emotion. It can come upon you quickly…so unexpectedly, and yet when it passes it is usually difficult to remember why you considered it such a big deal. Life is too short to spend time being angry about something so small that it usually disappears almost as quickly as it appears.

I read almost daily about some act of violence that occurred over 'road rage'. Someone does something, most often a thoughtless, inconsiderate act while driving, and it provokes another person into a response that is even more stupid. Why? Every one of us, at some time or another, has done something while driving that inconvenienced someone else. But was it worth injuring another person or their property…taking their life? I can't imagine anything that serious. Someone once said:

"Sometimes when I get angry I have the right to be angry, but that doesn't give me the right to be cruel!"

Don't get me wrong, I've gotten thoroughly agitated at some driver's foolishness. Who hasn't been cut off by someone who immediately makes an abrupt turn…when there was no traffic behind you? That is total nonsense that can make you mad enough to want to harm someone. But as one person wrote:

"Anger is one letter short of danger."

I tend to get bugged over little things… like people who leave their shopping carts in the middle of a parking place. Especially when they are ten steps away from a collection point. Now that is aggravating! And some of those people could certainly use the exercise! But a violent response…I don't think so. Besides, within an hour so I tend to forget all about it. Life is too short! I think about the old saying…

"Anger is like taking poison and waiting for the other person to die."

But, at the same time, there are legitimate things that <u>should</u> elicit anger. I feel war is one. War solves nothing! It never has...it never will. And yet, at any given time, there are several wars in full swing somewhere on the globe. So-called 'ethnic cleansing' is another. And yet it continues to be a problem around the world. Why would any people feel they have the right to kill off another people because they are different? And yet it has happened for centuries. In our own country it happened numerous times to our original settlers...the Native Americans. We can always seem to find some justification for these senseless killings. Regardless of the reason innocent people die or are chased from their homes, and their land. When will all this nonsense end? Where will it end? Bede Jarrett wrote:

"The world needs anger. The world often continues to allow evil because it isn't angry enough."

At the rate the climate is changing the day will come when there will be an even greater shortage of water. When will people begin to die because they have more water than their neighbors do?   I guess the answer lies in where we place our anger.   Perhaps we need less of it on the highway and in parking lots...and more of it directed toward the evils of intolerance and indifference toward human life.   What do you think?

"Sticks and stones may break my bones…"

Dear Reader: It is necessary for me to note here that I have been attempting to write this 'musing' for several years. Each time I felt prompted to attempt to sit down and write I seemed to run into a brick wall. Words seemed elusive. I just couldn't get it together. At long last the concern over the issue got the best of me. I decided that I could wait no longer…I had to get my concerns on paper.

* * * *

The well known old response we used to rebuff a person who was name calling or taunting us as children now has a sad, but important new twist. I believe few people would intentionally hurt a child. I still say this in the face of the fact that we seem to be hearing more and more frequently of cases where children are abused, even abandoned or killed by their parents. Parents harming their own children! Incomprehensible! Even harder to comprehend is the fact that churches in recent years have paid millions of dollars to victims of religious leaders who were guilty of physical abuse. It is hard to fathom how any adult could deliberately set out to physically harm a child, but such acts by people in positions of moral authority are beyond the pale.

Years ago, in my generation, some parents inflicted what they referred to as 'discipline' on their children. Sometimes this was a bit extreme, but after a brief cooling off period they usually regretted their actions. My own parents were God-fearing, church-going people…but they were capable of dealing out 'discipline' with a leather belt at what I felt was the least provocation. I remember those sessions well even after over five decades have passed. And I must admit that as a parent I have been guilty of doing the same thing to my own children. Not as often, not as severe, but by today's definition it could be considered abusive. I am in no way attempting to justify my behavior. I regret every occasion in which I let my temper get the best of me. Over the ensuing years I

have learned there is no excuse for ever letting things get that far out of hand.

That being said I am a bit concerned about
the way the young people are being raised in
today's environment. I see young children
doing some pretty mean things to each oth-
er-screaming and acting up in public, using
foul language, you name it. And I hear their
parents respond by saying "Johnny, you need
a 'timeout'" and then doing nothing. It is
no wonder the behavior continues or even es-
calates into violence. Clearly parents need
tools and training to help them with the difficult task of molding children's behavior into
acceptable forms.

However, the abuse issue today is real and
we need to give it considerable attention.
Not only is it wrong and harmful to our children, but it is a major drain on our nation's
economy. In conducting the research for this
piece I came upon some statistics that are
staggering. Dr. Suzette Fromm, Vice President
of ChildServ, a Chicago-based organization,
places the annual cost of child abuse at $94
billion! That's billion, with a B! Personally, I feel it is on the high side, but the
estimate is based upon a lengthy and credible
list of references. It includes every con-

ceivable cost that could be included in the broad category of abuse. I in no way want to minimize the costs associated with this aberration in human behavior. Whatever they are is unacceptable under any circumstances.

We need to understand what children are. I frequently remind my audiences that children are sweet, innocent spirits <u>on loan</u> to us from the Creator. They are not our personal property. They are not chattels. Perhaps most important of all, they are only loaned to us for a very short time period of time. We need every precious moment of that time to nourish their minds as well as their bodies. That doesn't mean they should not be disciplined when necessary. Even the Bible allows some room for discipline. But prudence should guide any act of punishment. Another bit of counsel is attributed to the carpenters who say, "Measure twice, saw once." In other words, think carefully before you act… make certain the discipline does not exceed the crime!

"...but words can break my spirit!"

Words are powerful tools. They can inspire, motivate and encourage. They can also do almost irreparable harm. As adults, most of us have developed mechanisms for dealing with input from others that may be hurtful or difficult to hear. As children, however, we are not able to sort out the motives of those who attack us, and our image of ourselves and our capabilities can be severely damaged by words said in anger by parents and significant others. Too many of us spend a lifetime consciously or unconsciously struggling to erase negative messages about ourselves planted in childhood.

I remember as a child hearing people say "Mary was an accident", or "John wasn't planned for, he just happened", or "If it wasn't for my kids I would have had a better job". I always felt sorry for these children. *It* would be tragic to go through life feeling as though you were unwanted.

In nearly every presentation I have made relating to this subject, participants will volunteer that a parent (and on occasion both parents) told them repeatedly as they were growing up that they were dumb, stupid, ugly, too fat, too skinny, etc. Negative messages heard as children can become internalized limitations. Any number of these people have said they never tried to get better jobs, or go for a better education, because they felt they did not have the mental capacity (or the personal appearance) to reach higher. Many of us are quite good at limiting our ability to grow and progress with messages created out of our insecurities. "I could never do that, because…" "If I ever tried that I know I would fail". Someone would laugh at me!" If these limits have their roots in ideas planted during childhood by those upon whom we depended for our emotional and physical well being they are particularly difficult to dislodge.

This also extends to the words tossed around among siblings. While these words can be just as damaging, they have a better chance of being forgotten in time. Siblings, as adults

at a family gathering, will be able to recall any number of mean and hurtful things
they said to each other when they were young.
Although they may laugh at the memory as
adults, as children it was not so funny.

This is not to suggest that mean-spir-
ited verbal abuse should ever be tolerated.
Children should be taught from an early age
to be supportive of one another. If they
learn this early in life it will be a valuable skill they most likely will carry into
adulthood.

It is critical that we continually support our children and nurture them with words
that are both supportive and geared to aid in
their long-term development. In the long run
our civilization will be the better for it.

What I've learned from Judge Judy

I find the courtroom television shows interesting. In all fairness I should include all the other judges in the title--Christina, Alex, Joe, and a host of others. The thing I find most interesting are the people who appear on these shows, and the situations they have gotten themselves into. Take for instance the 25 year-old woman in a case I saw not long ago. She was a single mother of *five children*...that's right...*FIVE!* She had borrowed three thousand dollars to bail her new boyfriend out of jail! And, of course he had not paid her back! When asked she said she had no choice in the matter, he had asked her for help. And besides, she thought they were going to be together forever. He responded that he never asked her for the money. She gave it to him as a gift.

I agreed with the judge that it seemed hard to believe a single mother of five could afford to make a gift of that much money. He remained unconvinced. The defendant said the plaintiff was mad because he was moving on with his life and had a new girlfriend.

In another case a young college student had taken her Pell Grant check and bought her boyfriend a $1600 set of custom rims for his car! He couldn't get them for himself because he had poor credit and, in fact, at the time he was unemployed! The young girl said she had no choice and besides, he had promised to pay her back in two weeks. She didn't ask where the money was coming from since he was not working, and it never occurred to ask why he didn't just wait for two weeks and buy them out of his money. He was under the impression the fancy rims were a gift. Of course they were no longer together and he had a new girlfriend.

In yet another case a 35 year-old woman had bought a cell phone for a life-long friend and put it on her account. The woman said she had no choice…her friend had no credit, but needed the phone to keep in touch with her kids and her boyfriend. The defendant claimed she had loaned the phone to her boyfriend and he was the one that ran up a $2000 dollar bill for the month. It wasn't her fault and she should not be responsible for the bill.

It is always of interest to me that there are so many of the cases, hundreds in fact that revolve around the misuse of cell phones! And the monthly bills these people manage to run up are staggering. Does anybody *work*? I ran a business that had smaller phone bills for an entire year!

In yet another case a woman couldn't get a credit card because of (ho hum) bad credit. It is encouraging to hear that some credit card companies actually review the applications! Anyway she asked her friend if she could borrow her card to go shopping. She needed diapers for her baby. The plaintiff shrugged...she had no choice...her friend had an infant that had to have diapers. The defendant took the card and went on a shopping spree. She bought clothes for herself. She took her boyfriend and several friends out for a fancy dinner. She paid other bills, too. One was a past due cable bill...nearly $400! And when the plaintiff saw the bill she was floored...the price of diapers had gone up! But the defendant swore she would pay the entire amount from her tax refund. When the tax refund failed to materialize the case wound up in court. On television, no less, in front of millions of viewers.

So what have I learned from Judge Judy…and the others? Well, for one thing, each of the plaintiffs claimed they no *choice* in the matter. They *had* to do what they did. The defendant had *asked* them to do what they did. I would like to point out to these folks that *everyone* has options in life! From these options we make choices. We can choose to give in to the other person, or we can choose to say 'no'. We always have a choice in the matter.

Throughout our entire lifetime we face options on a daily basis. These options may not always be obvious. Some times we have to look around for them--but there are options. Some options may be relatively simple--where we go to have lunch, what we choose to eat, what television shows we watch what time we go to bed. These are all simple, routine options. After we consider our options we make choices…we make decisions. And, for the most part, we live with those decisions.

Other choices are more complicated. Who should we marry? What car should we buy? How much should we spend for a home? How many children should we have? (Five still seems like a high number, but it is certainly a viable option for those financially equipped to feed, clothe, and educate that many sweet spirits.)

My intention is to point out that we should carefully consider our options and the impact they might have, before we make our choices. But once we make our choice...once we have made our decision...we will usually have to live with it, for better or for worse. Of course we can change our minds. We can eat somewhere else...we can go to bed later...we can trade in a car if it proves unsatisfactory. But some decisions are harder to reverse...once made they carry an obligation that needs to be fulfilled. Making decisions quickly, with little or no thought given to the consequences or the underlying assumptions can be at the root of lots of problems. Too often we resort to the court system to unravel the problems we create.

The more time we spend evaluating our options...and thinking through the possible consequences of our choices, the better our decisions tend to be over the long run, the easier they will be to live with, and the more contented we will be.

So thanks to you, Judge Judy, and all the other judges for pointing out to people, even indirectly, that they *do* have choices. And they should exercise more judgement before making decisions, rather than leaving the judgement to you.

Ghosts, Yellow Lines, and Sacred Cows

Why is there so much unhappiness in the world? Perhaps it is because people let outside factors influence their concept of success, and thus fail to experience the happiness they so richly deserve. I can't help but hearken back to my consulting days and several barriers I observed that frequently got in the way of organizational growth. I called these barriers ghosts, yellow lines and sacred cows. I used these terms to describe how the barriers originate, the problems they create, and how they should be resolved.

"Ghosts" are caused by events that took place in the past, but still have a negative impact on people and their perception of the world around them. I first encountered a 'ghost' many years ago. I had just begun an interview with a group of hourly people.

I explained that I had been brought in as an unbiased consultant to help the company find ways to improve performance and reduce production costs. I was interested in any ideas, suggestions, and comments that they might be able to contribute. Suddenly a rather elderly woman erupted. Her eyes were bulging and the veins on her face and neck looked as though they were about to explode. Tears ran down her face as she angrily choked out the words. "My boss said I was lazy, and I'm not! I've worked on the farm since I was three years old. I cooked and cleaned and took care of my ten brothers and sisters. I raised eight children of my own. And since I have been here I have not missed one day of work!" She pounded her fists on the table and shouted, "I am not lazy!"

Her fellow workers were shocked. I had interviewed all of the supervisors and could not believe any of them were capable of inspiring such rage. In my calmest voice I asked, "When did this happen?" Her answer stunned me!

"I have worked here for eighteen years...it was sixteen years and three months ago! It will be seventeen years this November 15th!"

The fact the supervisor in question had retired twelve years earlier, and had been deceased for over five years had no impact on this poor woman. But as much as she was angered over the remark, she had never mentioned it to anyone before that day. She had carried that hostility and anger with her every day of her life for nearly two decades!

This was an extreme case, but I have seen many, many examples of 'ghosts' over the years, people who have spent years being angry over incidents that in many cases were taken out of context. It is important to remember that as implausible or bizarre as these 'ghosts' may seem, they are very real to the person affected by them!

"Yellow Lines" are barriers, physical and/or psychological, that reduces personal productivity and effectiveness. I first recognized this phenomena in a manufacturing plant that produced automotive parts. The plant was rectangular with the main entrance and the time clocks at one of the narrow ends of the building. The parking lot completely surrounded the building. At quitting time the employees ran from all over the building to punch their time cards and join the mad dash around the building to their cars. To

prevent injury the company had painted yellow
lines around each department and staggered
quitting times.   Then they set up strict
rules that no employee could cross the line
until the end of their shift.

I noticed that when I talked to individuals they would try to maneuver me to a point
where they could put their foot on the line.
Some of the more aggressive types would actually step across the line as we talked. They
were constantly arguing over who would leave
the department to get supplies. Any excuse
for violating the lines. "They have tuna fish
sandwiches in their vending machines and we
don't! I want to go over there and get one
for lunch!" As the people worked they actually stared at the lines. At the end of the
day fistfights were fairly common and griev-
ances were at a record level. I suggested
to the client that they were losing too much
productivity because of the lines. I rec-
ommended that they paint over the lines and
put time clocks at each side of the building.
This would allow the people to park closer
to their department when they came to work
and leave in a more orderly fashion. It took
a full a full year for the client to adopt

the suggestions. When they made the changes productivity immediately increased by over 30%!

"Sacred Cows" are operations, policies, and procedures that are considered off-limits to scrutiny by external resources. They are often beliefs that people choose to hold on to for whatever reason. They may have been true in the past, but in their minds they are still true today. When I met with a client for the first time they would often say something like, "Don't worry about the Widgets product line, that's our big money maker!" or the big boss would say, "Don't worry about Marketing, that was my old department!" or "These procedures were set up by our founder!"

When I heard something like this it was often the first place I would look for problems because it was usually an area no one else had scrutinized, often for years! For instance, the Widgets may be considered the big money maker because some of the production costs associated with that product were being charged to other product lines. When costs were more appropriately distributed the Widgets may not have been the company's bread and butter after all.

Another example that comes to mind was a large machine shop with over 200 separate workstations. Each operator kept track of his or her production on an hourly basis. One morning I was meeting with one of the officers when a young woman walked into the room carrying an enormous stack of bound reports. She gave the officer a copy and left. I would guess the report was at least an inch and a half thick. The officer thumbed through a dozen pages, wrote a few numbers on a notepad and threw the report into the wastebasket.

The next day I was meeting with another executive when the scene was repeated. On the following day it was repeated in the office of another executive. This time I asked about the report. I learned the report contained the hourly productivity of each machine by each individual worker. The officer explained that he was only interested in the production of one product. The rest of that report was useless to him. It turned out that ten years earlier the founder had established the practice of keeping records in this manner.

Further investigation uncovered the fact that this young woman came to work at 4am. She gathered up all the data, made copies, bound them, and distributed them to each of the officers by the time they came to work. She was an unhappy camper because she had to get her two children up and to the babysitter at 3am so that she could get to work and do these reports that no one cared about.

In addition, it turned out that she was using a dozen reams of paper each day and making nearly 6000 Xerox copies (at .025 cents per page), to produce the report. I suggested they make a few changes. The young woman began to come to work at 8am. She gathered together the data each officer needed and had it on their desks before 9am. Everyone was happy (including the babysitter) and the company realized a savings of over $10,000 per month! All that over a 'sacred cow' that was over a decade old.

Now, how might these phenomena apply to your personal life and the lives of those around you? Well, "ghosts" are harmful because they tend result in a great deal of unhappiness and often-unnecessary anger. It is difficult to try to reason with a person who has a 'ghost'. Merely telling them the incident was unimportant, or that it happened a long time ago will not exorcise the ghost. Suggesting they just forget it will not make it go away.

I instructed the supervisors I trained that
the most effective way to eliminate a ghost
is to *listen* intently to the person. When
they are finished *acknowledge* that you have
heard and understood, and if the incident
ever occurs again they are to come directly
to you. Getting it off their chests and out
in the open seems to help diminish the intensity.

If an event from the past just will not
go away, it may be time to seek professional
help to work it through. Talking about the
experience and sorting out its meaning is a
step toward exorcising the ghost.

In our personal lives the 'yellow lines'
we paint around ourselves can be just as limiting and destructive. Probably the most
serious are the self-limiting doubts we have
about our abilities. Each of us, at one time
or another, has walked away from a situation
because we felt we did not have the where-
withal to overcome it. We just felt we did
not have the ability, or the knowledge, or
the stamina to get beyond the problems presented by that particular situation.

The problem is that this kind of behavior can become addictive. Backing away from
problems and challenges becomes easier when

we construct 'yellow lines' around ourselves. As each new situation arises it becomes easier and easier to back away. We may reason that we aren't smart enough to overcome the situation--it will take too much money--we don't have the time, or whatever. We are too young...or too old.

When you paint 'yellow lines' around yourself there will always be some reason why you can't confront the situation. However, overcoming obstacles brings new personal growth. Each victory over an obstacle or problem makes us stronger, more knowledgeable, and better prepared to tackle even larger problems and obstacles. And most important of all, many of these obstacles are really opportunities in disguise...just like the immediate increase in productivity experienced by my client.

Some self-doubts may be the result of criticisms from the people close to you, such as friends, co-workers, or even family. Mark Twain wrote:

"Keep away from people who try to belittle your ambitions. Small people always do that, but the really great make you feel that you, too, can become great."

Some failure is to be expected. It is part of life. Thomas Edison wrote:

"Many of the failures are people who did not realize how close they were to success, when they gave up!"

My advice to you is, eliminate any self-imposed barriers in your life. Don't accept limitations until you have given the problem your very best effort. A 'sacred cow' might be some belief or practice you choose to hold on to that, in the long run, may prove detrimental to your personal growth and development. It could be a religious or political belief you have held from childhood that you haven't challenged and still accept as truth, even though things have changed; a prejudice or bias that you cling to that has never been reviewed or challenged; an addictive practice that remains in place unchallenged. One or more of these 'sacred cows' could be present in our lives and in the lives of those around us.

How we address the 'sacred cows' in our lives is our own business. But it is important to consider that if some area of our lives is causing us grief or unhappiness…or is holding us back in some way, we should not be afraid to challenge it and take any necessary corrective actions. Anything that prevents us from realizing a full, rich, abundant life should be recognized, challenged, and resolved. Only then can we realize our birthright of a successful and happy life.

I would like to share with you an experience that to some degree ties together all of these barriers. I was meeting with the general foreman of a client company. In the middle of our discussion he received an important phone call from one of his department heads. As they talked I happened to look out of the office window. It looked out over an area of the plant. I noticed a wall that had been built between two of the workers. It was made mainly of cardboard boxes, thin strips of wood, and wire. It was at least twelve to fifteen feet high, and was a total eyesore.

When he finished his conversation I asked the general foreman about the wall. "I'm curious about that partition out there. There are no sparks or metal filings flying around. What is its purpose?" He looked out the window, shook his head and laughed. "If you look closer it is actually two walls. Those

two men were the best of friends for years.
Then one day they had a disagreement or something. The next day one of them put an empty
refrigerator carton between them. The next
day the other fellow put together a couple of
boxes that were a foot or so higher than the
original one. A day or so later the first guy
added a foot or two to his wall. This continued until it reached its present height." He
paused for a moment. "I've thought several
times about taking it down, but it does help
morale a bit." "How so?" I asked. He pointed
to two men walking down the main aisle toward
the restrooms. It was late in the day and
both men appeared tired. They were slouched
over and their gait was more like a shuffle.
They were not together...one was several feet
behind the other, but their reactions were
the same. As they approached the wall they
both smiled at the absurd sight...their shoulders straightened and their pace picked up.

The general foreman turned to me. "You see
what I mean? Everyone thinks it is so ridiculous they have to laugh. So at a certain
level it is a morale booster." He looked
at me for a moment as it he were reading my
thoughts. "I know, it is ugly and it could

be a hazard. How do you think is the best way to handle it?"

I thought for a moment. "Today is Monday. Tomorrow morning I would tell each of them that first thing Friday morning the wall is coming down. I would tell them that if they can't resolve their differences you will have to move one, or both of them, to another department."

On Wednesday afternoon I was walking through the department and noticed the wall was gone. I poked my head into the general foreman's office. "I guess you couldn't wait until Friday?" He laughed, "No, Tuesday afternoon they asked if they could use my office for a few minutes. In less than an hour they came out and tore down the wall themselves." He paused, "I think the way they handled it is a lesson for all of us. I think it might just be a morale booster for everyone!"

I think the lesson for us today is this… when we build a wall we often have to put forth a great deal of time and effort to justify it. When the wall is one we have built around ourselves in the form of unhelpful and limiting beliefs, it might be time to take it down.

Time

"Dost thou love life? Then do not squander time, for that is the stuff life is made of."
Benjamin Franklin, **Poor Richard's Almanac**

Time is one of the most valuable commodities, and how we use it will determine the relative success…or failure…of our entire earthly existence. We each have a certain amount of time given to us at birth, but in most cases vast amounts will be squandered before we ever realize its true value.

Time is inelastic…it does not expand and stretch, and yet some people learn to get far more out of each second they have been allotted. They cannot stretch their time; they just learn how to invest it more efficiently.

"It has been observed, that those who have the most time at their disposal profit by it

**the least. A single hour a day, steadily
given to the study of some interesting subject, brings an unexpected accumulation of
knowledge."**

William Ellery Channing

We have all manner of devices and technol-
ogy at our disposal to help us use our time
more effectively. Millions, no, billions of
dollars are spent annually on gadgets to help
us plan each day…and yet valuable seconds,
minutes, even entire hours slip away completely unnoticed and underutilized.

To most of us time is given little attention until it is gone. We spend our early
years eagerly anticipating the passing of
time…waiting for Christmas…our birthday…sum-
mer…the Senior Prom ...graduation. We are
always in anticipation of an event that lies
on the distant horizon and that seems to approach at a snail's pace.

We spend our later years wondering where
our time went. Mourning the passing of the
months and years…awed by the way in which the
passing of time accelerates with the dawning
of each new year. Julia Cameron, in her book
"The Right to Write" said:

"The myth that we must have 'time'—more time—in order to create is a myth that keeps us from using the time we do have. If we are forever yearning for more, we are forever discounting what is offered."

I believe this thought encapsulates the essence of what time is all about. Too often we grouse over an event that took place in the past...an ill conceived comment...a failed relationship...a missed opportunity, etc. In doing so we miss out on the joy we should be experiencing with each new day. The future will come soon enough. We must glean from each new day all of the promise it offers to us. Abraham Lincoln wrote:

"The best thing about the future is that it comes one day at a time."

Abraham Lincoln

As you sit quietly and watch a sunrise, especially after a summer rainstorm, you feel as if the moment will never end. The clouds seem to barely move...as if they were tiny wisps of cotton pinned to a deep blue sky. Even the birds seem stilled by this spectacle of Nature. Time seems to become frozen in this most perfect moment.

But it is an illusion. Slowly everything begins to change. The clouds thicken and drift into larger clusters. The soft pastels along the horizon begin to brighten. The sun begins to assert its authority. It casts its light on the distant mountains and the orange and russet peaks separate from the shadowy valleys. A new day begins in earnest. The birds begin to chirp. The rabbits and squirrels and other mountain creatures begin their daily quest for food and shelter. The magic of this still-life work of art suddenly becomes a whirlwind of activity. A brand new day emerges and time is once again on its endless march toward tomorrow. Someone once wrote that whatever you accomplish today is important because you are investing one day of your life to achieve it. In reality time is not as much a commodity as it is capital to be invested prudently.

"The proper function of Man is to <u>live</u>, not to exist. I shall not waste my days in trying to prolong them. I shall <u>use</u> my time." (*Emphasis added*)

Jack London

The deer and the antelope don't play!

Well, at least they don't play together. Actually they sometimes play together, but they don't enjoy it. They play together reluctantly. Even though they are first cousins and, on occasions are actually confused with one another, they aren't real buddy-buddy.

That may seem strange to some of you who grew up listening to the song "Home on the Range", which clearly points out that the range is where deer and antelope play. I guess, if they were going to play, they would of necessity have to play on the range. I mean, have you ever heard of deer and antelope stadiums...or arenas...or playgrounds? Believe me, I have conducted a great deal of research into the matter and I have not found a single facility, of any sort, devoted to the recreational needs of these poor creatures. They are essentially on their own to create not only places to hold their competitive events, but to devise the games themselves.

The games, such as they are, must be played on the honor system…there are no licensed or sanctioned officials to preside over the contests. If they could at least organize into recognized leagues they would be able to get proper officiating. They could also get corporate sponsors and politicians to build them stadiums. They could get revenues from advertisers. In time, I'm certain Nike and the others would create footwear, jerseys, and the like to generate even more revenue. Every kid would want to be the first to wear a pair of deer sneakers. They would spend big bucks (no pun intended) to wear their favorite player's jersey and number.

Stadiums would be packed with fans…but on what days would they play? Weekends have been pretty much dominated by college and pro teams…even Monday nights are taken in the fall and winter. That leaves the midweek…but not especially the best days for drawing big crowds. There would be conflicts for people who have to work the next day…kids have school…and homework, and so forth.

But I'm getting way ahead of myself. All

of this is not likely to happen any time soon. First, deer and antelope are going to have to learn to play together! They don't necessarily need to passionately embrace the concept, but they are going to have to recognize some benefit to playing together. And right now they are light years away from reaching any form of agreement...even as to the most basic premises.

Now I've talked at length to both sides and here is the gist of the problem. First of all while they may appear to be similar, they are not. The antelope feel the deer play too rough and do not like to play by the rules. They feel the deer commit excessive fouls...and occasionally try to sneak a large elk into the game as a 'goon' just to pick fights and injure the antelope star players.

The deer, on the other hand, feel the antelopes are 'wimpy'. They feel the antelope are more fragile and timid. The deer contingent believes that they are far superior athletically and desire games of skill that demand strength, endurance, and stamina. They feel the antelope are more cerebral...they want games that require more thinking and reasoning...and less physical prowess.

When you attempt to get the two species together to work out some form of compromise the meetings invariably erupt into shouting matches. Each side accuses the other of only wanting games in which they can dominate...of only wanting to establish rules that favor them rather than rules that are fair and just. Several such meetings had to be adjourned abruptly when hooficuffs broke out. It seems hopeless at this point.

Frankly, I don't feel that the deer and the antelope are ever going to play together again...at least for the foreseeable future.

But that doesn't mean those of us who are deeply concerned should give up. We should not abandon hope of ever getting the two sides together. Perhaps if we could get the best minds in the sporting world to apply their creative energies to the problem we could once again see the deer and antelope playing together in friendly competition.

Coulda, woulda, shoulda...

A few weeks ago I was talking to a new acquaintance who has been retired for several years. He had asked me what I talked about when I spoke to groups. I mentioned several of my more popular topics including "Pathways to PURPOSE". He scoffed and said, "I don't want anyone to tell me how to live my life...I'm happy just the way it is!" At the time I was a bit taken back, but since then I have given his response a good bit of thought.

I have presented that program numerous times to groups ranging from corporate executives to 'lifers' in several of our rankest prisons. It is a frequently requested presentation and I have been paid handsome fees to present it. I have always assumed that it was requested so frequently because most people have an interest in the subject. I still believe that. However, I also believe that in any audience there are a few people who are not passionately interested in the subject. With that in mind I always make every effort to present my material in a non-critical, non-judgmental manner. I trust that presentations made in such a way provide food for thought for the participants in the days and weeks that follow.

But in a way my friend makes a good point. No one likes to be told they should be dissatisfied with any aspects of their life. Even if they are dissatisfied they don't necessarily want to hear it from someone else. I can certainly empathize with their position. However, I would be unhappy with myself if I didn't take every available opportunity to make my audience aware of the fact that their PURPOSE is important both to them and the people around them.

I would not like to think that anyone I've spoken to over the last thirty years would reach the end of their life's journey with a severe case of the 'coulda, woulda, shoulda' disease. That is the disease that causes people to reflect over their life and say "I coulda." 'Coulda' implies that the resources, talents and opportunities were in place… the individual just chose not to act.

'Woulda' means the person believes they would have followed through if conditions were different. Perhaps they feel the right combination of resources, talents and opportunities were not in place at the proper time…but they 'woulda'.

The saddest are the people who feel they 'shoulda'. Too late they realize that they had the resources, talents, and the conditions were right and they did not act. They are the folks that feel the greatest remorse. They regret their procrastination or reluctance to take action. The very fact that a person could live their entire life and, at the end, have some regrets is not unusual. I guess that to some degree we all have regrets of one sort or another. Who among us could look back and feel they had done everything perfectly? Conrad Hilton said:

"Achievement seems to be connected to action. Successful men and women keep moving. They make mistakes, but they don't quit."

I guess my greatest motivation when speaking is to get people to realize that in most cases it is not too late to right any wrongs, not too late to accomplish something they

might have left unfinished. I would like everyone to leave my presentations with a 'can
do' attitude...recognizing that "There are still
many things I can do!"   For me, the essence
of life is having no regrets and no unfinished
business, at the end of the journey.

Picking up Rocks

For years, before I ever thought of moving to this special place, I began to pick up a rock on each visit. I felt that in some way it helped me stay connected to the land. The rock didn't have to be large...most were smaller than the size of a fifty cent piece. With the exception of a few they were not in any way spectacular or unique. I guess it is similar to picking up seashells when walking along the shore. I never got too excited about collecting seashells. I always felt that extracting the little creatures from inside the shells was a smelly, messy experience that I didn't much enjoy. Picking up a small rock and slipping it into my pocket as I hiked always seemed like a much simpler process.

There was one time when I did go a bit overboard. While doing a consulting project at a coalmine outside Price, Utah I be-

came interested in rock polishing. I bought
a polishing machine and set out to find some
rocks to polish. I was told I could find some
agate in dry creek beds. Early the following
Saturday morning I set out on an expedition
to find some of those beautiful native rocks.
I fully expected that finding agate would be
much like panning for gold. I thought that
after a day's effort I would be lucky to
harvest a pocketful of stones. Imagine my
surprise when I parked above a small arroyo,
got out of the car and stepped on an agate
the size of a softball. That day I found at
least fifty pounds of agate, all shapes…all
sizes…all colors. In the course of two weekends I amassed at least a hundred pounds of
rock. It was only when I was packing to return home that I realized how impractical it
would be to attempt to take that much rock on
an airplane. Reluctantly I eliminated all
but about twenty pounds of my treasure. That
Christmas I presented gifts of homemade jew-
elry to all my friends and relatives. Some
were pleased. Some could have cared less.
But I enjoyed the experience more than I can
say. The finished gems were smooth and shiny.
I thought they made exquisite gifts! I still

have a few of the stones in a drawer along
with my cufflinks and bolo ties.

When I speak about the magic that surrounds
this area I always counsel my audience to find
a spot where they can sit alone in complete
solitude for an hour, just to be alone with
nature and their most private thoughts and
concerns. If they have some particular is-
sue--concern over a relationship, finances,
or even a health problem, they should share
it with the Universe. Speak aloud, if possible. But release the concern or issue to the
Universe with the expectation that it will be
dealt with by powers beyond their comprehension. Be assured that in the proper time,
the issue will be resolved.

When I left New York I seemed to have some
anger issues that I had a difficulty explain-
ing. I attributed it in part to the angry-
type characters I had played in several films.
I thought it might also be the result of the
environment created by the constant noise
and crowds that are a part of the Big Apple.
Because of this I was having a difficult time
writing. I felt it was a 'writer's block'.
It was quite troublesome. So much so that I
consulted a psychic reader. She assured me

that my problem was not a block, but rather the fact that I had become less receptive to the environment around me. I then went to my favorite meditating spot and there I sat for several hours. During this time I gave the problem to the Universe. When I left I felt as though a heavy weight had been lifted from my shoulders. Almost immediately the ability to create returned and I was again writing.

I suggest this technique to each of you. When an issue stands in your way...when a problem interrupts your Earth Walk, sit for a time in a quiet place. I now believe such places exist even in large, noisy cities. But find one of these spots and sit alone and meditate for a time. Release your issue to the Universe. In a short time you will find the problem is resolved and you can resume your Earth Walk unencumbered by the burden imposed by the issue. As a remembrance of the occasion and this special bond you have made with nature, pick up a small rock and take it with you. Carry it with you every day, or place it some place where you will see it often. In that way you will always remember that concern, and you will recognize the moment in which it is at last resolved.

Any number of my personal issues have been resolved in this manner, so I believe in it with all my being. Give it a try…what have got to lose besides the issue itself.

Entitlement

I guess to begin with I should describe the prospective from which I am writing this piece. I am sitting alone on a mountain in one of my favorite places to think and write. I have a pocketful of beef jerky and a canteen full of water. I am not sitting in some ivy-covered building where pontificating about entitlement and empowerment might seem more appropriate. I mention this only because, from this perspective I can discuss my thoughts as I see them. No one else is involved. So if any person...or group...gets ticked (and I expect they will) so be it. I am at an age where I have seen a good slice of living, and feel compelled to throw out my thoughts as grist for the mill.

First of all, I believe that the concept of 'entitlement' is becoming harmful to this country of ours. People on both ends are misusing it. On the one end we have the people in power--politicians, businessmen, even some religious leaders--who feel they know what is best for all the rest of us. More and more we have seen excesses and abuses of their exercise of power. Politicians creating laws <u>they</u> don't have to follow or getting us involved in wars that their sons and daughters won't have to fight. They tell us we need to sacrifice even as they are profiting from the whole mess.

At the same time many of our so-called business leaders take obscene personal wealth out of their companies through questionable practices while demanding cutbacks from the very people who struggle to keep the organization afloat. It seems to me we are rapidly losing the ability to 'grow' organizations in this country…to take an idea and build it into a strong and healthy organization that provides employment opportunities to the masses. I know I am generalizing a bit, but it takes a heap of good, strong, growing companies to undo the damage of an Enron or a Worldcom.

It seems to me that the powers that be in all fields, including the field of religion, often create smoke screens that distract us from the real issues. The media contributes to this. They are quick to grab any little sound bite they can use to make a deadline. Few of them seem interested in digging deep enough to get the whole story, especially when it involves a major advertiser, or contributor to a political party, or a current darling of Wall Street.

Any real exposè comes well after the damage. Criticize anything in this current environment and, if you are heard, you might be labeled as 'unpatriotic' or 'anti-country', or even 'anti-God'.

Well, believe me, I am not one of the above. I love my country. I still love my country, even though some of our current policies would be an embarrassment to the vision our forefathers had when they developed our founding documents. I believe their vision was a nation where people in power used their power and wealth to build a strong nation...a vital, growing nation.

I'm not a man with a fancy education, but I am what used to be called 'a God-fearing man'. And deep in my soul is the conviction that people who label themselves as 'men of God' and 'doing God's work' had better do so only after some deep searching of their own

souls. Taking on the responsibility that
goes with the assuming of these labels is
not something a person should take lightly.
If you <u>really</u> believe in God you must know
how he deals with those who use His name in
vain.

But those in power are not the only one
with a misplaced sense of entitlement. There
are many others who feel they deserve certain
entitlements just because they exist. They
expect…no, rather they <u>demand</u> entitlements
and empowerment they haven't earned. They
demand 'respect' when they haven't given any
to anyone else.

If we are ever going to get back on track
as a nation that the rest of the world can
look up to and admire, we must rid ourselves
of this sense of entitlement. We must contribute our talents and our positions to make
the world a better place to live and grow.
At the same time we must not take from the
pot more than we contribute. In this way the
pot, the world's aggregate wealth, will continue to expand and there will be plenty for
everyone for many years to come.

The Stream

As I walked along an unfamiliar trail I came upon a stream. Large cottonwood trees shaded it and the sun was at an angle that made it difficult to judge the depth and the speed of the current. I stood there for several long moments, just enjoying the beauty and serenity. One could easily pass an entire day just sitting there and reflecting upon life. For a time I was tempted to do just that. But I had places to go and things to do that at the time overshadowed the prospect of a tranquil and thoughtful experience.

I carefully considered my options. Should I try to cross the stream or retrace my steps? It is my nature to want to move forward and to not travel the same ground twice in the same journey. However, I could not estimate the depth of the water. Nor was I certain how fast the water was moving. Could I easily walk across...or would I be knocked over by the current? My inability to make a decision at that moment caused me to sit on a large rock and reflect on the possibilities that lie in front of me.

I suddenly realized that the situation in front of me was strikingly like a decision I was facing in my life's journey. I was in the process of considering several business deals that were much like the unknowns of the stream. If I stepped into these agreements would they provide a pleasant experience and meaningful progress as I continue my Earth Walk...or would I find the experience to be unpleasant ...disappointing...even detrimental to my long-term growth. There was not a great deal of money involved...certainly not enough to ruin me financially. But none the less a degree of risk was involved.

I needed to cross that stream, but at what cost? Understand, my dignity, my ego was not a particular consideration. If I got wet, if the experience was less than pleasant it would not be a great calamity. It was probably not a life-threatening situation. But at the same time I needed to know if the risk was justified. Was whatever lies beyond the stream worthy of such a risk? Would others

benefit if I took this risk? Were there ben-
efits beyond my rather limited view? I continued to meditate for quite some time. I
finally concluded that the business deal was
probably worth the risk. And now I had to
decide whether or not to proceed across the
stream. I thought about it for a few more
moments and then I made my decision. As it
turned out the experience proved to be well
worth it. The views were spectacular!

And, I might add, it took less than an hour
in the hot Arizona sun to completely dry my
clothing.

The Ant Colony

The other day, as I sat in my garden, I noticed hundreds of ants scurrying between two of the flagstones. As I watched them I realized they were building an anthill. In a short time they became a bit of a nuisance. They began to run into my sandals and up my legs. For a time I merely swatted them away, but being one who prefers to work without distractions, I eventually took action. I went to Home Depot and bought a canister of ant powder. When I got back to the garden I spread a coating of the lethal powder over the area between the flagstones. For awhile I watched, but not much seemed to change. The offenders continued to scurry about...running in and out of the coated area. I went back to work, still somewhat annoyed that the powder did not seem to have an im-mediate impact upon the problem.

The next morning was different. Only two ants were moving about frantically. One came

from the east with the early sunrise. The
other was running across the flagstone from
the opposite direction. Both were in a fren-
zy. For very brief periods they would even
venture over the edge of the flagstone into
the fringes of the white powder. Then they
would race back across the flagstone, only to
return again and again.

At first I thought it was sort of humorous.
But then a sickening thought crossed my mind.
Had I committed what amounted to a holocaust…
an Armageddon of sorts? Had I created a di-
saster in their tiny world that could never
be rectified? I mean now they can't relocate.
They can't just pick up and move to another
garden somewhere and start anew.

Did they have time to ask what they had
done to offend the giant ogre with the canister of death? Had I become a terrorist of
sorts to the tiny creatures? Had I created a
day of infamy in the ant world? Did I create
a 9-11 in their world?

9-11! Again I thought about that day, the
difference it made in my life, and the difference it *could* have made. At the time I
was living in midtown Manhattan. On Septem-
ber 10th I was on jury duty in New York City
a few short blocks from what would become

Ground Zero. I was the fourth alternate on a jury selected to decide the fate of a woman accused of a number of petty thefts and credit card scams. I had expected to be excused because her crimes had mostly been committed in my neighborhood. No such luck!

After sitting around for several hours on the morning of the 10th we were informed the woman had accepted a plea bargain and we were excused. Otherwise I would have been in the proximity of the World Trade Center at the time of the terrorist attacks. Instead I was on a train headed to White Plains to run some errands. About half way to White Plains a woman on the train listening to the news on her transistor radio heard the towers had collapsed. She panicked and began to scream that the country was under attack and that we were at war!

When I arrived in White Plains I hurriedly finished my errands and returned to the train station. There I was advised by a police officer that service to the city had been cancelled until further notice. The sympathetic officer told me that one train was leaving for the city with medical personnel. He quietly suggested I get on board and not say anything. However, the train stopped at a place called Mount Vernon where authorities advised us that the train was being checked for bombs before it would continue to the city. We were asked to leave the train and told that only people with appropriate credentials would be allowed to reboard.

I was new to the area and had no idea where I was and how I could get back to my home on East 37th Street. It occurred to me that if I could get a bus to 125th Street in Harlem I could walk the ninety blocks to our apartment. It was a French couple that helped get me on a subway headed for 69th Street. At that point the train was stopped and everyone had to disembark. Okay by me--now I'm only 30 blocks from home! But luck was with me. Across the platform was a train headed for 42nd Street. I got on just as the doors were closing. It was a short trip, but eventful. Tensions were higher than normal. People were yelling at one another. A fight broke out in the over-crowded car.

When the train finally reached 42nd Street I was relieved. I was as close to home as I could get. Cellphones were not working and I began to worry about my wife who worked in the Empire State Building. When I arrived at the apartment I found her safe and sound. We embraced for a long time. It was a day the entire nation will never forget.

But what about the ants? By now the entire site is completely free of any activity. Even the two remaining ants had also disappeared. Did they give up their search? Did they have to take up residence in another colony? Did they, in complete despair, enter the destroyed structure and perish with the others? I will never know. I can only hope that they can somehow find it in their hearts to forgive the big ogre with the canister of white powder. I know for a fact that, upon reflection, he wishes he had overlooked their minor intrusion into his thoughts.

Saying Goodbye

One of the toughest things a person has to do in the course of their Earth Walk is to say goodbye. People say goodbye many times in their lifetime. Some good-byes are relatively temporary: when a child leaves for school each day, when a spouse leaves for work, when friends leave a restaurant after a lunch. Good-byes are more difficult when the person is leaving for a longer period of time and/or they will be further away--when a child first goes away to college, or when a person is leaving on a long journey. I have learned that even when a loved one is as close as a telephone, good-byes can be a bit stressful. Being separated from my wife for the better part of a year while she completed the final year of her contract was at times more difficult than either one of us could have imagined.

We also have to say goodbye to places and things. At one point I had to say goodbye

to the city of Pittsburgh, where I had lived
for some 35 years and to the home where my
wife and I had lived for eight years. The
next years meant two more good-byes to homes
where the stay was brief but many memories
were made.

The strange thing about saying good-bye
to a home is you also have to say good-bye
to some of your 'stuff'--that large pile of
minutiae that accumulates each time you get
ready to make another move. This includes
books, clothes, furniture, and just plain junk
that you are sure you can not live without.
Eventually you reach the conclusion that you
don't have room in your new residence, or it
will not fit in with the new 'stuff' you will
inevitably buy when you get there. Then you
have to say good-bye. Maybe it is sold in a
yard sale, given to relatives, or given to
Goodwill. These good-byes aren't usually
tearful, but there is the inevitable empti-
ness--at least for a little while.

However, as I think about it, the saddest
good-bye is the one that never gets spoken. It
happens quite frequently, I suppose. Someone
you didn't particularly like, someone you had
a beef with, dies. When they are gone you
realize the problem you had with them wasn't

all that serious, that perhaps it could have been resolved with more conversation over one more cold beer or a good cigar.

But that conversation can never take place. The other person is gone. Gone forever. That chasm can never be bridged. The conflict may have been a big deal to one or the other person. Chances are it wasn't. It was just something that came up between two people and stayed there until it was too late. What is the answer? I wish I knew! I've had my share of these situations, but I can't say that I had an answer when the time was appropriate. The difficulty of letting go of things; a house, a favorite piece of furniture, a car, pales in comparison to the good-bye that never gets said to the other person.

There will always be another piece of furniture, or book, or car. But that person will be gone forever, and they can never be replaced. Think about it, I know I will!

Weaving the Tapestry of <u>your</u> Life

Each of us has the opportunity to create our life. To ignore that opportunity is to surrender control to the forces of chance and happenstance. Many people nowadays seem to feel their spouse, their boss, and even their children, have more control over their lives than they do. What a shame! You have only one life to live. Just one. To surrender it to someone else's whims and control is ludicrous. Worse than that…it is foolish and shortsighted. It is your life! Take control of it and make from it whatever you wish. Create your own personal tapestry.

Throughout much of my adult life I have helped organizations and individuals shape their own destiny…to weave their own personal tapestries. In all fairness I do not deserve the credit for most of these success stories. These 'tapestries'…these life changes, al-

ready existed. There were there all along.
I was merely the catalyst for bringing them
to the surface. It was a matter of helping
the organization, or individual, recognize
it for themselves.

In essence that is what I am suggesting
to you--find the spirit that lies within you.
Release that spirit so that you can weave
your life's tapestry. Create your own destiny. Have the life you want for yourself.

Begin by spending some time alone. Set
aside some time to sit quietly…away from all
distractions. Reflect. Look inside yourself.
Get acquainted with your inner person--the
real you, the you that was created for this
special point in time to live a particular
life of service and purpose. When you find
that special person take the necessary steps
to actualize their potential. Weave your
tapestry.

I've always liked the metaphor of the Old
Master Weaver and how he goes about the task
of creating his tapestry. First he sits
quietly before his loom, contemplating the
design he wants to create. At the appropriate moment a vision will come into his mind
and the complete design will unfold before

him. He will visualize the 'spirit' of tapestry.   Only then does he begin his work.
He first selects the 'warp".   The warp is the
vertical cords that are strung on the loom
to give the tapestry the strength and dura-
bility.   In your personal tapestry, the warp
are those things you need to accomplish to
bring forth the spirit of your life.   What
tools are required?   Do you need more training? More education? Better health, clearer
focus?   Are there specific skills you need to
develop?   Whatever these foundational conditions are, they are the 'warp'...the vertical
cords of your tapestry.

Once your warp is in place you can begin
to think about your 'weft'.   The weft is the
horizontal cords the old Master Weaver weaves
through the warp.   The weft provides the flex-
ibility and uniqueness to the fabric.   You
could say that the weft provides the origi-
nality to the fabric...the qualities that make
it different...and special.

In like manner your personal tapestry takes
shape.   You need to decide how each of the
necessary elements, or accomplishments, of
your life must be achieved.   Here you begin
to add your own uniqueness...your own personal

touch, or flair. As you achieve each accom-
plishment the tapestry takes its own form
and texture. It separates from all the others…it is completely unique.   It is your
life's tapestry! Yours alone! Never to be
duplicated! One of a kind. As your life's
tapestry is special, you are also special.
    Consider the words of this poem:

The Plan of the Master Weaver

Our lives are but fine weavings
That God and we prepare,
Each life becomes a fabric planned
And fashioned in His care.
We may not always see just how
The weavings intertwine,
But we must trust the Master's hand
And follow His design,
For He can view the pattern
Upon the upper side,
While we must look from underneath
And trust in Him to guide…
Sometimes a strand of sorrow
Is added to His plan,
And though it's difficult for us,
We still must understand

That it is He who fills the shuttle,

It's He who knows what's best

So we must weave in patience,

And leave to Him the rest

Author Unknown

The Search for Inner Peace

Look around you...on the street, in your workplace, even in your home. Everywhere you look you see people who are sad or troubled in some way. They often lack a sense of fulfillment because they are disturbed by some extraneous issue...real or imagined. Some of these issues may be life threatening...some downright silly. Nevertheless they are issues that distract people from the sheer joy they should be experiencing in their daily lives.

So, how does a person sort through the chaff to find the grain of wheat? There is an old story about a little boy who desperately wanted a pony. One day he finds himself in a room filled with horse manure. Eagerly he picks up a shovel and begins to feverishly shovel the manure out of the room. When his father asks what he is doing, he answers, "With all this horse manure, there has to a pony in here somewhere!"

Life is sometimes like that story. Sometimes we have to work through a lot of unpleasant junk to find our pony. Sometimes,
hidden in all our troubles, there is a gem--
a diamond in the rough--an experience worth
all the effort. An experience we can use
as a foundation for a complete and exciting
life.

How can we make this all possible? How can
we learn to get beyond the garbage? Well,
the first step is to find the real you…to find
that inner person that is your source of power. Finding your inner person is a huge step
in resolving any and all life issues. To
realize who you are, and what you are, will
open up the windows and allow the sunshine to
penetrate the darkness.

I found my source of power through a form
of informal meditation. I used to have a
small dish garden with a tiny waterfall. It
helped provide for some valuable quiet time
in which I think through problems and issues
of concern. Now I am blessed with a back-
yard that looks out over mountains that range
from the Mingus mountain range to the beautiful red rocks of Sedona. I spend many hours
working and meditating in this very special
environment. At times in these quiet moments

I attempt to find my Inner Person. In these moments I can sometimes get a glimpse of the pathway I must take to find my life's PURPOSE. It enables me to know that indeed I <u>have</u> a PURPOSE and I must continue to pursue it with all my being.

N. Gorden Cosby refers to this experience as the "central silence". He says:

"To reach that place is to be at home; to fail to reach it is to be forever restless"

In these periods of silence you often have an opportunity to discover who you are...and what you are to be doing. In the silence you will frequently find you are in the presence of your Creator. You need a time of inner silence to hear His voice...and to absorb His counsel.

You may use another technique for finding your Inner Peace. You may even refer to it by another name. The only point I wish to make is that seeking that sense of personal Inner Peace is well worth the effort you might put forth. It is an important aspect of living a complete and happy life. So take the time to find a quiet spot where you can sit alone. Think of any issue you are currently facing.

Regardless of whether it is a problem with a relationship, a financial problem, even a health issue…when you release it to the Universe you will find that in no time it will be resolved and you will feel more peaceful and happy. You will be one step closer to finding the state of being I refer to as Inner Peace. Give it a try!

"Far away in the sunshine are my highest aspirations. I may not reach them, but I can look up and see their beauty, believe in them, and try to follow where they lead."

Louisa May Alcott

Compassionate Compromise

We live in a time when everything seems so chaotic. There is conflict throughout the world…armed and otherwise. Nations…religions…races…creeds …communities…even families are engaged in heated disputes over issues, real or imagined, that separate them from their neighbors. I know this has been going on since the beginning of time, but because the world has become so small over the past few generations it seems to be more apparent than ever before. Most people involved feel there is no alternative…this is the only way. "It's my way or the highway!"

I know this may seem like an oversimplification, but at times it seems like there is no room for discussion…no room for compromise. And yet there are few issues so important…so critical…that a middle ground cannot be worked out if tolerance and understanding are applied.

I am reminded of the story of the lion and the unicorn. They were natural enemies, and yet in the story they learned to live together in peace and harmony. No two entities could be any more different. One a flesh eater, the other a vegetarian, and yet they could lie side by side in harmony. How is that possible? Nations or humans with superior intellect can't seem to accomplish that feat. National and religious credos seem destined to get in the way of any opportunities for lasting peace and harmony.

As a boy my father told me of an event in history involving these two creatures that illustrates the potential for compromise. In 1603 King James IV of Scotland became King of England, which effectively united both kingdoms under one rule. The Scottish Royal coat of arms had two unicorns supporting a shield. The English coat of arms was similar, but used lions to support their shield. When King James took over he created a coat of arms with a lion of the left and a unicorn on the right. This was a great compromise! Both animals are recognized as king of the beasts—the lion rules by might and power; the unicorn signifies rule through harmony.

Is it possible that as a society we could

learn to master the art of compassionate compromise?   Can we learn to sit together like
the lion and the unicorn?   If we are able
to compromise it will most likely begin by
learning to resolve issues affecting our own
personal lives.   Compromise does not mean
we have to give in on every issue.   It only
means that we have to find a common ground on
the issues that are critical to maintaining
successful relationships.   In this way, if we
really work on it, we can eventually achieve
lasting peace and harmony in both our personal lives and throughout our world.

And may this be the last word.

Printed in the United States
112188LV00002B/292-327/P